ABSORBING SPONGEBOB

Ten Ways to SQUEEZE

More HAPPINESS Out of Life

Steven Harriman

BERKLEY BOOKS, NEW YORK

THE BERKLEY PUBLISHING GROUP
Published by the Penguin Group
Penguin Group (USA) Inc.
375 Hudson Street, New York, New York 10014, USA
Penguin Group (Canada), 90 Eglinton Avenue East, Suite 700, Toronto, Ontario M4P 2Y3, Canada
(a division of Pearson Penguin Canada Inc.)
Penguin Books Ltd., 80 Strand, London WC2R 0RL, England
Penguin Group Ireland, 25 St. Stephen's Green, Dublin 2, Ireland (a division of Penguin Books Ltd.)
Penguin Group (Australia), 250 Camberwell Road, Camberwell, Victoria 3124, Australia
(a division of Pearson Australia Group Pty. Ltd.)
Penguin Books India Pvt. Ltd., 11 Community Centre, Panchsheel Park, New Delhi—110 017, India
Penguin Books (NZ), Cnr. Airborne and Rosedale Roads, Albany, Auckland 1310, New Zealand
(a division of Pearson New Zealand Ltd.)
Penguin Books (South Africa) (Pty.) Ltd., 24 Sturdee Avenue, Rosebank, Johannesburg 2196,
South Africa

Penguin Books Ltd., Registered Offices: 80 Strand, London WC2R 0RL, England

This book is an original publication of The Berkley Publishing Group.

SPONGEBOB SQUAREPANTS is a registered trademark of Viacom International, Inc. This book was not au-
thorized, approved, licensed, endorsed by, or created in association with Viacom International, Inc., or any
other individual or entity associated with the *SpongeBob SquarePants* television show, movie, or characters.

PRINTING HISTORY
Berkley trade paperback edition / October 2005

Library of Congress Cataloging-in-Publication Data

Harriman, Steven.
    Absorbing SpongeBob: ten ways to squeeze more happiness out of life / Steven Harriman.
        p.   cm.
    ISBN 0-425-20704-8
        1. Conduct of life.   2. SpongeBob SquarePants (Television program)—Miscellanea.   I. Title.

BF637.C5H367 2005
158—dc22

                                                                                            2005048222

PRINTED IN THE UNITED STATES OF AMERICA

10   9   8   7   6   5   4   3   2   1

Dr. Steve, the guy who wrote this book, was trained as a clinical psychologist. Watching every episode of *SpongeBob SquarePants* dozens of times with his niece, he realized that Sponge and his pals offer more savvy on how to be happy than a boatload of shrinks. So he squeezed a small ocean of that wisdom into this book. It costs a lot less than even one shrink in a dinghy and, hopefully, will cause the reader to smile.

To my dear niece, Lauren Emily,
for all the hours we've spent laughing with the Sponge.

ACKNOWLEDGMENTS

Grateful thanks to Ginjer Buchanan and Susan Allison at Berkley for bringing this book in and seeing it through; to John Morgan, F. Paul Wilson, and Nancy Lyon for their superb edits; and to my literary agent, Howard Morhaim, for putting us all together.

CONTENTS

THE 3RD WAY
HARD TRUTHS

THE 4TH WAY
ECONOMICS

THE 5TH WAY
TIMING

CONTENTS

THE 6TH WAY
FAMILY VALUES

THE 7TH WAY
THEOLOGY

THE 8TH WAY
GETTING ALONG
WITH OTHERS

THE 9TH WAY
GETTING ALONG WITH YOURSELF

THE 10TH WAY
MASTERING THE UNIVERSE

INTRODUCTION

Some of you might protest that cartoon characters are not real, and thus cannot be used to illustrate how to live.

If you don't think SpongeBob is real, why did you pick up this book?

Interestingly, only cartoon characters and humans, while they can teach many lessons, routinely refuse to let anything be a lesson to them.

This doesn't mean we can't *learn*. Obviously, we can, or we'd all go around wearing plaids with paisleys and carving our initials on the boss's desk. But we'd rather have a root canal than let our dentist talk us out of our jones for Snickers bars. We learn what we want to learn, and nobody but nobody "teaches us a lesson."

Actually, that's kind of neat in a way. We're stubborn,

we are. We have our pride. As do SpongeBob SquarePants, Squidward Tentacles (especially him), the money-grubbing Eugene Krabs, the slyly clever Patrick Star (for whom dumbness is at least partly a façade), and even Sandy Cheeks, the perspicacious underwater squirrel, who would rather get her best pal SpongeBob fired from his job than let him convince her they must stop practicing their karate. Squidward, having gotten lost trying to deliver a pizza for Mr. Krabs, spends a figurative forty days and forty nights wandering the undersea wilderness with SpongeBob, subsisting on raw coral, rather than believe that Sponge actually knows the way home, and that it's just over that hill.

Wisely, SpongeBob knows better than to try and make Squidward listen.

The number-one reason psychologists burn out and stop doing therapy is that only one patient in a thousand will actually listen to what the therapist is trying to get across. It takes around seven years to train the average clinical psychologist. Most of that time is spent drumming into these would-be do-gooders that a proper therapist, contrary to every instinct in his or her bones, never gives advice. (This is why if you ask your shrink what your dream about finding yourself suddenly naked in French class means, he or she will throw it right back at you: "What do *you* think it means?")

Sooner or later, of course, most psychotherapists, deprived of the satisfaction of getting their points across without actually giving any advice, succumb to the irresistible urge to flat out tell their patients what to do. (It should come

as no surprise that shrinks refuse to let seven years of graduate school be a lesson to them.) Then the patient goes out
and does the opposite and the poor, frustrated therapist
burns out with the sound of popping corn.

This book, *Absorbing SpongeBob*, is full of advice. In
nearly every eleven-minute episode of the show there is
some lesson to be learned, if only we would, if only we
could. Lessons about handling our fear, about heeding life's
little "stop" signs, about hard truths that are better learned
in books than from experience. SpongeBob and his friends
routinely dish out lessons on economics, the importance of
timing, family values, theology, existential stuff, and getting
along with yourself and others. We excuse this subtextual
moralizing because the lessons are delivered with a light
touch that never spoils the fun.

SpongeBob is such a good little guy that he might at
first seem not to need to learn anything. He is clearly the
bright and shining star of his undersea world. However, as
the visitor to Bikini Bottom quickly learns, Sponge's goodness is not the same as savvy. While it often seems that he is
not learning the lessons his actions bring on, he is a very absorbent fellow. The proof of this is that the way he lives has
resulted in a glowing inner happiness that can never be
dimmed for long. This is what we all want, right? Happiness. SpongeBob loves life. He is ready. His example pro-
vides good lessons for us all.

The reason this does not stop him from getting into
jams is that jams are an unavoidable part of life. SpongeBob
and the other inhabitants of Bikini Bottom are a lot like us,

only funnier, which is why they are real and alive despite being "only" cartoons. Funny is good.

And, hey—if you happen to be that one-in-a-thousand person so highly evolved you actually *can* let something be a lesson to you, this book is your chance to prove it.

THE 1ST WAY

HANDLING FEAR

1

DON'T SWEAT THE SMALL STUFF

Most everyone would agree that fear is a bad thing, especially when it happens to them. Different things scare different people. More precisely, cartoon characters and human beings are born with two different types of nervous systems that help determine what scares them. It's good to know which kind of nervous system we have, so we can use that mutant growth at the top of it (our brain) to finesse ourselves out of being afraid, and yes, this really is possible. Two episodes of *SpongeBob* will illustrate the two types of nervous systems, and then we'll move on to why (aside from how nasty and unpleasant fear is) it is both possible and important to be less afraid.

In an early episode of *SpongeBob SquarePants*, Squidward Tentacles, Sponge's next-door neighbor, unthinkingly tosses a shell out the window of his stone fortress house, which resembles one of those tiki heads from Easter Island, only darker and more sinister. The shell drifts over and lands in the front yard of SpongeBob's sunny orange, obsessively kempt pineapple home. Instantly, Sponge pops out of his pineapple, eager grin on his face, leaf blower in hand, power pack strapped to his square back. He fires that sucker up and, like all leaf blowers, it is noisy.

Among the many things Squidward can't stand is noise. Squid likes it quiet. He is always hoping SpongeBob and Patrick will go away for the weekend to a jellyfishing convention or anywhere at all so he can venture from his stone keep to sun himself in peace. So it should come as no surprise that when SpongeBob fires up the leaf blower, Squidward gets hopping mad, and with four legs he is a better hopper than most. (Squids outside Bikini Bottom have ten legs, some of which are, arguably, arms. That Squidward has only six arms and legs is no doubt related to the reason Mickey Mouse has only three fingers.)

Why does noise make Squidward mad?

Let's skip past the obvious—he doesn't like noise—and go to the not so obvious: Squidward gets mad because noise startles him, and startled is the first part of scared, and nobody likes to be scared.

Axiom: An angry male squid is nearly always, more fundamentally, a scared male squid. (Less true of female squids because it is more okay for them to admit they're scared.) Male squids, like the males of certain other species, learn at a very early age that they aren't supposed to show fear. It's unmalesquidly. So, whenever squids and this other species (hint: raised partly on playgrounds) are scared, an evil jinn transforms the fear straight into anger. But at its root, the anger is really fear, proving this hasn't been the digression you were beginning to suspect.

SpongeBob, unfailingly kind, doesn't mean to irritate, much less scare Squidward—which, with a dime, will buy Squid eight minutes on a parking meter.

Why is Squidward scared of a little, or even a lot of, noise?

Because he is an introvert.

For most people, this word evokes that shy, skinny kid in high school who kept to himself, wore dark clothes, had body odor, and, when spoken to, gave us a strange smile and sidled away. For others, the word is synonymous with "male engineer," who looks at his shoes while he talks to you. Female engineers stare you right in the eye and never blink. (The reasons for *this* sex-linked difference are beyond the scope of this book.) When "introvert" comes up in conversation, what we think of, in a word, is "shy." From here on, "introvert" means one of those two types of nervous systems shown on page 10.

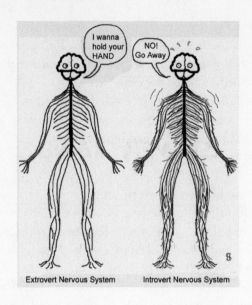

2

CLEVER HANS

The concept of introversion/extroversion has been around for hundreds of years. One of the first "modern" psychologists to get excited about the subject was Carl Gustav Jung, who lived at the same time as Sigmund Freud and liked to argue with him. But it was Hans Eysenck (1916–1997) who shined the bright sunlight of scientific research on introverts and extroverts. Fortunately, they did not burn up under his magnifying glass like ants on the sidewalk, but yielded lots of interesting information. What Hans discovered with his many experiments was that the brain and nervous system we're all born with varies a huge amount in how much stimulation it likes. At one extreme you've got people who come into this world determined to avoid a ruckus at all costs. Their nervous systems are easily overstimulated. These people grow up to become librarians, always shushing patrons who whisper, scratch themselves or drop their Kleenex.

People born at the other extreme would, if they could, come out of their mothers' tummies with boom boxes pressed to their little ears. They can't get enough stimulation. These people grow up to become car dealers who do their own commercials, standing there jabbing their pointing finger at you with every word they say and talking in a very loud and excited voice.

There's probably a bit more variety than that, but you get the idea.

Between these two extremes lie the rest of us. About 70 percent of us live on the extrovert side of the line, and the rest are slight to severe introverts. (If you are an introvert, you are probably wondering if "extrovert" should be spelled "extravert." Either way is fine. Try to relax.) Bottom line: When Hans Eysenck talked about introverts and extroverts, he was talking about how we're wired. Turns out, it's one of the most important things to know about yourself if you want to be happy.

As noted earlier, Squidward Tentacles is an introvert—an extreme one.

How, you say, can a gourmet cook and clarinetist be an introvert?

With rare exceptions, Squidward cooks and plays the clarinet only for himself (and not because no one else could stand the screeching). Enter Mr. Krabs, owner of the Krusty Krab diner, which serves Krabby Patties (the cannibalistic implications of which are another story). Suffice it to say,

Mr. Krabs hired Squidward to "squid" the counter of his diner, where the show's extras shamble up to place their orders. (The extras are mostly goofy-looking fish, with an occasional crustacean or mammal thrown in.) Krabs hired Squidward for this job not because Squid is a people-loving extrovert, but because there are only so many characters in the show, and since SpongeBob is the fry cook, Squidward has to field the orders. It might work better if the extroverted Sponge were to work the counter and Squidward the grill, but it wouldn't bring nearly as many laughs.

Squidward's surly and dismissive attitude toward his customers and the little digs with which he disses them (no one gets these bon mots because no one much listens to Squid) are an obvious sign of the poor cephalopod's crying need to be alone, like the writer Flaubert, in a completely white room with his head wrapped in white towels to keep out the noisy and distracting world. Note how the sarcastic remarks (anger) tip us off to the fear beneath—of being overwhelmed by noisy breathing reality, much of which is too real for Squidward.

What lessons are in this for us, assuming we are among the rare geniuses who can let something be a lesson to us?

First, in your approach to handling fear it's important to know whether you are an introvert or an extrovert. Do you like to be alone with your thoughts a lot? Do the little tags they put in underwear chafe you? Would you rather read a Patrick O'Brian novel than ride the high seas in a three-masted man-o'-war? Do you know if your socks are on the wrong feet?

You are an introvert, my friend.

Do you play the radio or TV when you're alone in the house? Do you like to go to four-hour meetings at work where everyone tries to talk at once and there's at least one spitty fight? Can you sleep through a 2 A.M. party in the next apartment, where rejects from *Animal House* sing "Ninety-nine Bottles of Beer on the Wall" at the top of their lungs? Do you think roller coasters are great fun? Did you fail to notice how "extrovert" was spelled and couldn't care less?

You, my friend, are an extrovert.

Thankfully, most of us are somewhere in between but, bottom line, the more introverted you are—that is, the more sensitive to the stimulations of life—the more easily chafed, startled, and generally fearful you will be.

3

GETTIN' DOWN

Does the extra fearfulness of introverts mean they are cowards?

Au contraire, as Gary the snail—the tall, dream version, in his scholarly robes and vast library—would say. "Gettin' down" may mean the exact opposite to an introvert as it does to an extrovert, but who is braver: those who must discipline themselves not to jump every time the furnace comes on, or those who wonder, as Captain Quint rakes his fingernails down the blackboard, why a third of the people in the room have turned the color of cottage cheese? You extroverts, who see no reason to let go of the rope when you fall off your water skis, are born with your thick skins. You had nothing to do with it, so we introverts will give you zero credit.

Hmmm. If sensitivity to stimulation is hard-wired, doesn't that mean we introverts are doomed to suffer nights of torture when the party starts up next door, to flinch every time the cat hawks up a hairball?

If you're expecting "no," sorry, the answer is yes.

Unless we decide to do something about it.

Knowing we are prone to sweat the "small stuff," we can put ourselves where there is less small stuff to sweat. We can give the poor cat hairball medicine. We can move just out of town, where the next house is far enough away that a party won't wake us, and the rent is probably cheaper (assuming it won't cause a daily commute that is more overstimulating than the occasional party next door). Or we can seal the noise away with double- or triple-pane storm windows that can be opened when there's no loud party, and buy one of those little machines that cover any leftover noise with soothing sounds like the surf, or gentle rain, or J. Lo combing her hair. We can quit our job as a bullfighter and instead translate books from English into pig Latin. We can wear soft socks, and cut the tags out of our boxer shorts, bras, slips and T-shirts. We can learn and practice relaxing. Of course, most of us won't, because we'd rather suffer a nervous breakdown than take advice from some silly book.

A final word before we move on to what scares extroverts. We can't control what nervous system we are born with, but we do have some say over how we live with it. Some people with extrovert nervous systems might come across as shy because they don't care to be around people. This could be because they find the rest of us too *un*stimulating (boring). Such people might even be confused themselves about what they are. If you are like that, but you love to swim with the sharks, rest assured, you're a born extrovert, and knowing it will help you squeeze more happiness out of life.

Likewise, there are plenty of introverts out there we'd never suspect were born screaming out pleas to retreat back into Mommy's warm safe tummy. Unlike Squidward, they don't freak out when the neighbor starts up his leaf blower they just move to a quieter room and put on a Yanni CD. They like to party, though not every night, and we don't suspect they are introverts because they look us in the eye and make good conversation. They like to talk about fascinating us rather than boring old them. We don't suspect they are introverts because we don't see them go home after the party and drink a glass of warm milk and read for an hour before trying to sleep so that their overstimulated nerves have a chance to settle down. These introverts have what we call social skills. Learning these skills has made being around people more rewarding and, thus, less overstimulating for these exemplary introverts. They have used their brains to outwit their spinal cords and peripheral nerves. Extroverts can prefer sailing a boat around the world alone to being with people because of all the excellent chances the voyage gives them to pit themselves against the stimulating seas and weather and to brag later that they did it without help. By the same token, introverts can like to party down because they've become so practiced with their social skills that they don't find a party overstimulating. We don't have to go around being what we're born, not even Squidward.

Proof: When Mr. Krabs wants to add entertainment to

his diner to bring in more customers, and thus money, who volunteers? Not the extroverted SpongeBob. Squidward, that's who. He dreams of being the master of ceremonies of a variety show that will be a big success and make everyone admire him. Why would an introvert care if he's admired? Because almost no one wants to be lonely or lightly regarded. So when Mr. Krabs calls, Squidward answers, because his learned desires trump his natural fear. For the night, at least, he has overcome his nature.

4

DON'T SWEAT
YOUR CRITICS

SpongeBob, as noted earlier, is an extrovert. Does this mean he is never afraid?

He wishes.

Extroverts might not jump at noises, or flinch if the shower comes on too hard, but they can be scared, too. What scares them tends to be different from what scares introverts, but scared is scared.

Let us now look at this flip side, to use a fry cook metaphor, of what tends to overwhelm the inborn nature of an extrovert—SpongeBob, to be precise—resulting in fear, panic and hilarity.

Being an extrovert, SpongeBob is not the kind of fry cook you never hear from, hidden away back there in the kitchen we'd rather not see, wearing an apron with enough grease to pomade a poodle, and looking like that stoop-shouldered, world-weary guy who slung hash on *M*A*S*H*. For one thing, SpongeBob is bright yellow, and his apron, like his kitchen, is always sparkling clean, in part because he is (as the theme song says) absorbent and porous, and he also knows how to swing a mop. As a fry cook, SpongeBob excels, and he is justifiably proud of his skill at making Krabby Patties, the aforementioned pièce de résistance of the Krusty Krab. On most days, the citizens of Bikini Bottom crowd in to savor his skill with this coveted burgerlike food, blissfully unaware of its possibly sinister origins.

And then, one day, in comes the sour and bloated Bubble Bass, self-styled food critic of Bikini Bottom. SpongeBob, the supremely confident extrovert, is ready. He is sure that Bubble Bass will find his Krabby Patty beyond reproach. He watches eagerly as Bubble Bass chomps down on the patty.

Bubble Bass, in the snidest of ways, crushes him. You forgot the pickles.

SpongeBob is stricken. Nothing in his experience has prepared him for this inexplicable failure to please a customer. He falls apart. He tries over and over to construct the perfect Krabby Patty, getting the ketchup, the mustard, the patty, the cheese, lettuce, tomato, and pickles in the right order. It's no use. He's lost it.

SpongeBob might not be afraid of the sound of a leaf blower but, gregarious and crowd-pleasing fellow that he is, he is terrified of scorn and rejection. Rude old Bubble Bass didn't just scorn SpongeBob, he did it in front of a crowd of customers. Turns out extroverts have fears, too, and nothing less than panic drives SpongeBob to recover his lost gift.

But he can't, he just can't, and finally, he gives up.

In the next instant, miraculously, he remembers how to do a Krabby Patty, and his whole life knits back together.

Actually, it's not miraculous, it's boring old science.

When SpongeBob gives up, his shoulders sag, his head droops, he looks more boneless than even a sponge. In a word, he relaxes. Another axiom: We can't be tense and relaxed at the same time. Scared = tense. Ergo, relaxing is a good way to fool the fear into leaving your body. Once SpongeBob isn't scared anymore, once he has given up and let go of his frantic efforts to reclaim his talent as a fry cook, it starts coming back to him. Why? Because he gave up? No. Because he *relaxed*. As the Bene Gesserit witches in *Dune* never tire of saying, "Fear is the mind killer." Frank Herbert, author of that novel, knew what an anxiety/performance curve looks like.

It looks like this:

21

For the graphically adept, a quick glance tells all. For the rest of us, a somewhat more lingering glance is allowed.

A little fear helps us do better—up to a point.

Say you've been asked to give a talk at the annual meeting of the American Phlegmatic Society. You say yes. If you have no concern (let's call it that for now) that you will do a splendid job, well, maybe you're right, providing you've done the same speech dozens of times. If not, you have what we call hubris, which might lead in the extreme case to you showing up fifteen minutes late and giving an off-the-cuff speech about postnasal drip, not realizing that these folks are laid back rather than phlegmy. Being laid back, they will probably take your weird and clueless presentation well enough, but whether you realize it or not you will have bombed.

If, on the other hand, after agreeing to speak you have some concern that maybe you ought to prepare, you'll read up and find out that phlegmatic means of slow and plodding temperament. You'll find out other things about the people in this society. Because you have a little concern (now let's call it fear) about whether you can do well and impress these stolid folks, you'll prepare some appropriate remarks, rehearse them, dress nicely on the appointed day, swallow a few times before going onstage, then do right well.

If you are scared of talking in public, always have been and believe you always will be, but you said yes because you want to date the person who asked you, you might do all the things in the above paragraph, go onstage on the big day, and tank because your shoulders are so stiff you can't turn your head and your mouth is as dry as dust and your knees are smiting one another and your mind *is totally blank*.

You, my friend, have reached the dread far valley of the anxiety/performance hill.

It may seem we're talking about an introvert here, and introverts in general will probably start out higher on the fear-of-public-speaking axis than extroverts, but there's a point on that axis where extroverts can be scared, too.

And it is also true that an introvert who has polished her interpersonal skills and practiced socializing and likes people may actually start out lower than (ahead of) an extrovert who fearlessly fails to prepare and ends up dodging hurled tomatoes, because it's the American Bilious Society, and laid back they are not. So bear in mind that introverts can triumph where extroverts fail in this little equation.

The key for both types is to reach the right level of fear—call it edge.

An edge is natural and desirable. You've practiced and rehearsed and learned and written a good speech and you *will* remember it and give it smoothly *unless* you fail to handle your fear.

This may seem a bit like that Gary Larson cartoon (how we miss him) of the people on the elevator, five or six folks of what passed for normal in Gary's world, men with inflated legs and slouchy postures, women with beehive hairdos and cat-eye glasses. These good folk just want to go up or down and get out of the elevator. Then the guy walks on with his pet lion and says, "Don't worry, you'll be fine, as long as he doesn't sense fear." (It may have been a brace of lions, or they may have been cheetahs, but you get the point.)

The cartoon is funny because you can tell from the

faces of the people on the elevator that at least one of them is going to freak. Most of us will never face a lion on an elevator, but SpongeBob's dilemma is all too real and possible in many daily lives. Most of us are on some job or other, and extrovert or introvert, we don't want to screw up. In this case, SpongeBob didn't screw up because he was afraid. He was supremely confident. But once he thought he had screwed up, it was so scary to him that he panicked and lost it, and made matters much worse than they should have been.

But how, you say, can I not be afraid when I am afraid?

You can relax. Shrinks teach this to people in therapy—how to think soothing thoughts as you feel where the tension in your body is, and tell those muscles, one by one, to relax, until you get more and more boneless and, in extreme cases, fall down drooling on the floor, whereupon the lion steps over you in disgust and goes on its way and you have *won*!

This works in the nonlion cases, too. You can probably learn it without the shrink, but if you can't, it might be worth a few sessions. The shrink will love you because you actually *can* take advice, and his or her head won't have to explode, and you will be happier because you'll be less scared, and therefore more capable. . . .

Unless, of course, you're afraid of shrinks.

5

DON'T BE AFRAID
OF CHANGE

Face it, the only change most of us like is the kind we find under our La-Z-Boys. In part, this is because some change is obviously bad, like getting in a car accident, or being thrown out of the house by our parents because we refuse to get a job, even though we're twenty-seven. Strangely, even though lots of change is good, like when the doctors finally saw the cast off your leg, or your boss gives you a raise and a promotion, humans and cartoon characters tend, on the whole, to fear change. The times when change sucked tend to loom large and bias our thinking.

Let's use an episode of *SpongeBob* to explore the two big factors that might lie beneath this bias.

It all starts in the underwater habitat of Sandy Cheeks, squirrel and "friend" of SpongeBob. It's never clear whether

SpongeBob is fully aware that Sandy is female, despite the fact that she wears bikinis on occasion. Since SpongeBob is watched by children as well as adults, romance and sex are kept to a tasteful, allusional minimum. Sponge and Sandy have tea parties, but they also practice karate together, and when they spar, Sandy usually wins.

In this episode, Sandy is going on vacation. She asks SpongeBob and Patrick to take care of her land-type pet, Wormy. This particular worm lives in a jar on a twig, not in the ground, which is our first clue as to what's going to happen. Sandy leaves with carefree good-byes. Patrick and Sponge find inventive ways to play with Sandy's little pet and end the day rhapsodizing over their love for their new best friend.

When they return the next day, instead of Wormy they find a butterfly in the jar.

They are startled. The butterfly flutters from the jar. Startled becomes confused as bits of the chrysalis at the bottom convince the two worried petsitters that the butterfly killed Wormy. As the butterfly lights on SpongeBob's helmet full of water (which he must wear in the air-filled dome), its bizarre features are greatly magnified—a hooking proboscis and eerie compound eyes.

Startled and confused become scared.

After running around in panic, SpongeBob takes out his trusty soap bottle and blows a bubble that captures the "monster," as he and Patrick call it. In this bubble the butterfly escapes the dome. First the Krusty Krab diner and then the whole of Bikini Bottom are terrorized, not by the butterfly so much as by the hysterical panic-mongering that's spread with share-the-pain relish by SpongeBob and Patrick.

Of course, we humans would never act like SpongeBob and Patrick did when they saw the butterfly. Change is all around us, a true constant in life. We've learned from our many experiences with it that it is not automatically to be feared. For example, if a helicopter suddenly lands on our lawn and three or four people come rushing at our door and pound on it, we do not hide under our beds or reach for the shooting iron. We open the door and cry out in glee, and accept the big check for ten million dollars from Publishers Clearing House that is going to change our lives forever and ever.

Or, if we haven't seen the TV reenactments, maybe we fill them full of lead before they can hand over the loot.

Axiom: It is not so much change we fear as "The Unknown."

Suppose the only context in which we've seen helicopters land and people rush a house is those giddy Publishers Clearing House reenactments. When the choppers touch down on our lawn, we might rush out and run at the DEA agents with manic glee and get shot full of holes by the deadly weapons they have brought along, because they fear the unknown, too—this charging maniac suspect—and then it turns out they've come to the wrong house and everyone is very sorry, except us, because we're dead.

See what can happen when you don't *know*?

Some slightly more common examples: You need to move to a different town. Or you're starting a new job. Or you are about to meet for the first time your half brother the ex–army sniper your long-gone father produced in his fourth marriage. Or, in order to get that first date, you have resigned yourself to the fact that you must go up to the object of your desire and ask for it.

Well, maybe you'll just stay in your old town. As you get nearer and nearer to deciding on the new job, the old job bites less. When your half brother rings the doorbell, you lie very still on the bathroom floor and don't answer. Rather than risk rejection, you resign yourself to a life of lonely celibacy.

Fear of change, fear of the unknown.

The cure for fear of change, which is really fear of the unknown, is knowledge—both of the unknown and of yourself and how your brain works in these situations.

Knowledge is obtained by studying and learning.

Bummer. We're scared of that, too.

But here you are, already reading this, so just read on a little further and get a valuable tip on fear of the unknown.

6

GO AWAY CLOSER

Most of life's looming changes aren't Publishers Clearing House checks or being shot dead by DEA agents, but somewhere in between, with potential for both harm and good. Again, boring old science to the rescue: The people that have studied "mixed-bag" changes (which are the most problematic ones) have found that the behavior of humans facing such possible change can be illustrated with a simple machine called a stymiepetcatulator, which you can easily build at home with a few pieces of plywood and a common house cat. (Cats larger than a house cat are not recommended.)

Anyone who has a "pet" cat has seen it stroll over to be petted, and then stop, maddeningly, just out of arm's reach. It is helpfully illustrating the "freeze point" even without

the bother and expense of building a stymiepetcatulator. While the cat is farther away, it imagines the nice feeling of your fingers scratching its head. As it gets closer, it begins to fear that you will pick it up and dress it in doll's clothes and take flash pictures that will blind its sensitive retinas for an hour. It freezes.

And that's us, trying to decide whether to take out that second trust to build separate bedrooms for our kids. Whatever change we both want and fear, as we are farther from it we want it more than we fear it. This causes us to approach it until the fear line crosses above the want line and, suddenly, we fear it more than we want it.

Why?

No one knows. It's just the way we are. We could say that when it comes to the crunch (freeze point), humans tend to be more scared of pain than hot for reward. That describes it, but doesn't explain it. The important thing to know is that it is natural, as you get closer to the change you both want and fear, to fear it more and want it less. Clinging to this knowledge is what enables you to boogie on past that freeze point and close the deal. Because you will have read this book, you'll know that the logic that caused you to want the thing in the first place probably hasn't changed, and that your fear is increasing because this is what happens when a human nears the freeze point. So, instead of lying there, paralyzed, on the bathroom floor, you muscle up and answer the doorbell.

Or not. It's up to you. The freedoms for which our forefathers shed their precious blood include the freedom to be a yellow-bellied coward. Is this a great country or what?

The other thing, besides the above tip, that will help you past the freeze point is, as noted earlier, more knowledge about the change itself. The more you can find out about the thing you both want and fear, the better the decision you can make when you reach the freeze point.

If you need further inspiration, SpongeBob and Patrick did seem to learn a lesson from the Wormy/Butterfly experience. In another episode, they rejoice when an egg they have been tending hatches into a chick. Leaving aside the likelihood of underwater chickens, maybe they are pleased because they feel the chick is cute, whereas their distorted view of the unknown butterfly was scary. Or maybe it's because Mrs. Puff, their Boating School instructor, prepared them in advance (offscreen) for the hatching. Learning from a teacher is something we all resist at least to some degree. But the bottom line is, whether we learn from experience, or from a book, or from a teacher or a shrink, knowledge—of the way our minds work, and of the change we're looking at—is the best way to reduce fear of change and take the plunge you were sure at the start would bring you greater happiness.

STOP SIGNS

THE 2ND WAY

7

LEAVE WELL ENOUGH ALONE

Much as we might hate stop signs, one reason the L.A. freeway is so scary is that it has none. Face it, sometimes we need them. Call it the yo and yo of decision making—knowing when to floor it and when to hold it. The next few chapters will focus on how SpongeBob and his friends handle various little stop signs in life, and how we can turn their triumphs and goofs into greater happiness for ourselves.

Around the age of two we become fascinated with "No." It becomes our answer to every question, no matter who's asking. It feels so good to say no, so. . . . *powerful*. *Mwahahahaha*. Some folks get stuck in this stage. They grow up to be referees, blowing their little whistles and sipping our boos like nectar.

Thankfully, most of us get past this infantile crush on

"No" and decide it's a bad word, especially when it stops us from getting what we want.

Our aversion to stop signs is perfectly understood on a certain small island in the Caribbean. This tropical paradise boasts in its travel brochures that it has no stop signs—a siren call to haters of gridlock everywhere. The island shall, of course, not be named here, lest we all rush down at once and cause two-hundred-car pileups with our rental Nissans.

Well over a dozen episodes of *SpongeBob* squeeze laughs from the perils of blowing off stop signs. One way people and cartoon characters do this is by failing to leave well enough alone. Visualize SpongeBob and Patrick sitting at a spot beside Squidward's tiki tower, their favorite place in all the world for playing noisy games. Today's noisy game consists of speaking into bubbles as they blow them. The bubbles drift back and forth; the two pals pop them to hear the messages, then laugh like maniacs. High in his tower, Squidward is annoyed by these outbursts of mirth. What should he do? Should he do anything?

Stop signs. Love 'em or hate 'em, it helps to know one when you see it.

Suppose a mail flyer offers us a free three-day vacation in sunny Florida. Some fine print suggests we will have to listen for several hours to a pitch for waterfront condos in the Okefenokee, where alligators are waiting to eat Ed (our hamster). If we take the freebies and then say no to the condo, we'll be made to feel like we swiped money from an offering plate at church. If we cave to the pressure and put ten thousand down, there's a chance we'll get the 'gators, not the condo, and never see Ed again. In fact, there are so many downsides to what is neither free nor a vacation that no one would ever accept such an offer, right?

Right. That's why the flyers keep coming.

Let's return to our annoyed squid. He could close his window and not hear Sponge and Pat, but that would be out of character, not to mention the end of the episode. Instead, he blows some snide bubbles of his own, disguising his voice to sound like Sponge and Patrick. His insults get the two buddies riled at each other. SpongeBob and Patrick hotly dissolve their friendship and stalk off. Squidward cackles with glee.

Enjoy it while you can, Squid.

What is the stop sign Squidward might have seen, if only he'd taken time to think? It's right there in the situation. All he had to do was put it into words, just form it into a cautionary thought, like this: "As long as SpongeBob and Patrick have each other, they don't need me to keep them occupied. Do I really want to change that?"

Now it's too late. Sponge and Pat are each going to need a new best friend, and who is right there at hand? Squidward. He'll find the idea of being fought over by the two about as appealing as a plate of calamari. Should have thought of that earlier instead of missing the stop sign.

8

ANGLES AND DEMONS

Another stop sign we often miss is the one that warns us not to press our luck. In 1810, Napoleon Bonaparte sat astride Europe, his empire at its zenith. Fifty million subjects sucking up to him, servants cutting his corn off the cob and turning his socks right-side out every night, no commuting in the morning because he worked at home. The original Napster was sitting pretty, and no one dared call him Shorty as long as a guillotine was waiting out back. So what did Napoleon do but invade Russia, lose five hundred thousand men, look like an idiot and plummet into a tailspin that led to exile and one of the longest palindromes ever constructed: Able was I ere I saw Elba. Backward or forward, it comes out the same—invading Russia clearly seemed a good idea at the time, but instead Bonaparte turned himself into what may be the most sobering example in history of not leaving well enough alone.

So how do *we* tell when *we* should stop pressing *our* luck?

Mr. Krabs faces just such a test when he closes the Krusty Krab for the night and informs SpongeBob he's off to play poker with Plankton. Sponge is shocked. How could Krabs enjoy playing against his archrival, owner of the Chum Bucket restaurant? Mr. Krabs yukkingly confides that Plankton is a terrible poker player. "I've been beating him for fifteen years," Krabs crows. "He *never* wins."

SpongeBob's worries melt away and he yuks it up right along with his boss, never dreaming that he will end up having a bigger stake in tonight's game than Mr. Krabs. Hey, if Krabs beats Plankton every time, why worry, right?

Apparently, neither SpongeBob nor Mr. Krabs realizes there is a branch of science that would help them at this moment, if only they had even a little knowledge of it.

Remember trigonometry?

Not the word, what you learned about it.

No?

Don't worry. Trigonometry won't help. We can use it to figure out the angles of a polyhedron but not of our lives, where knowing the angles really counts. Geometry teachers of the world, we love you, but was it really worth making us sweat through sines and cosines in high school when one out of a thousand of us would ever use it in the real world? Admit it, wasn't trigonometry just one big tangent? Even the word is off-putting, suggesting tapeworms and the metric system. Why trig, when another science course would have offered us way more help against the demons of the real world?

They should have made us all take probability.

As the name suggests, probability is the statistical science that can tell us how likely things are to happen. Wouldn't that be important to know? Probability is one of the few science classes that even people who fear science classes would like.

Probably.

And yet, rarely is it required in high school, and you don't come near it in college either if you major in most liberal arts. Trig teachers, congratulations on your powerful union. Statistics teachers, call Karl Rove.

The danger of never learning probability is that we will grow up believing the fundamental building blocks of logic are words—that whoever puts together the most persuasive verbal argument for a cause must be logically correct. As Eve's experience in the Garden of Eden proves, this notion is tragically flawed. (More on that in chapter 9.)

Not that language isn't wonderful. Without it, we'd have to rely on charades to tell our trigonometry teacher the dog ate our homework. Indeed, as this book proves, one can even fashion a career of sorts out of arranging little squiggles of words on paper. The problem with language is that it can sound logical when it's not. How else could humans once have believed Earth was flat, supported on four big pillars on the back of an enormous turtle swimming through the heavens?

Where the fungible logic of language hurts us most is

in the training of our reporters and journalists. With a few notable exceptions, nearly all of them major in English or some other liberal art. They go on from there to help shape public opinion and influence our personal decisions on such things as whether a newly discovered risky medicine we're taking is worse than the risk we'll face if we stop. So it sure is great that the few science classes our reporters had to take back in high school taught them squat about understanding such issues.

If Mr. Krabs had known anything about probability, he'd have had second thoughts about his *loooong* winning streak against Plankton. He might have decided not to press that incredible string of luck.

What's that you say? He shouldn't be betting anyway?

Okay, so you never go near casinos. That doesn't mean you don't gamble. There are plenty of risks in everyday life where it would be a big help if you could figure out whether you should press your luck. Suppose you've had three kids, all boys. You've always wanted a daughter. Should you try again for a girl child or content yourself with your three fine lads? (No, it is not all right to make the youngest wear dresses until he is old enough to beat you in a fight.)

Surely, if you've had three boys in a row, the odds go up of you having a girl next time, right?

Well, let's look a little closer at that. What was the probability on your wedding day that you and your spouse would proceed to have three boys in a row? Try solving that problem with trigonometry and you'd get a chart that looks something like this:

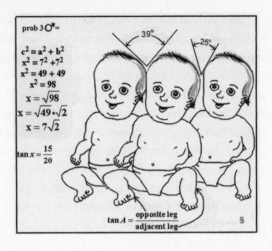

Can't decipher the chart? That's because trigonometry is clueless on how to help you solve this question.

Probability to the rescue (rousing trumpet fanfare). We'll start with the probability of having one boy. We can figure this out whether we've taken a course in probability or not. There are two types of babies, male and female, and it's not a bad guess from looking around that there are about as many males as females. So our best guess is that everyone has a one-in-two chance that their first child will be a boy.

So what were the odds of you having three boys in a row? You simply need to multiply the odds of having one boy—½—against itself three times. If you're interested in why we multiply ½ times itself, good for you. Go buy a beginner's book on probability, find out, and consider yourself one of the geniuses. Meanwhile, the rest of us have done the math on our calculators and found out that the odds of having three boys in a row come out to .125. This means twelve and a half couples out of a hundred would be expected to have three sons in a row and no daughters (or vice versa).

Fairly small odds, huh? Yes, indeedy. To figure out the likelihood of having four boys in a row instead of the three boys you've had and that girl you hope to have next, you multiply ½ times itself four times. This gives you 6.25 couples out of a hundred. Those odds are really low—terrific!

Too bad they have nothing to do with your question, which is what are the odds your next kid will be another boy?

They are exactly fifty-fifty.

If you're saying "Huh?" right now, you need to get that book on probability. In it, you will learn not only answers but how to ask the right questions. No matter how many boys you've had in a row, your chances that the *next* child will be a girl are exactly what they were in the first place and every time after—one out of two.

If Mr. Krabs had read up on probability, he'd have known that no one is so bad at poker that they lose every game for fifteen years. He'd have known Plankton was setting him up, and that he shouldn't bet SpongeBob's fry cook contract, because that's what Plankton was after all along.

The lesson we may draw (or reject) from Mr. Krabs's bad decision is that there are lots of go/no-go decisions in life where your gut instinct alone will steer you wrong. Knowing a little science can help. Should you act on that online stock tip that might take you from 5 percent annual earnings to 15 overnight? Or let that guy who came to your door blacktop your driveway, cash in advance, for a quarter of what the general contractor asked? If you remodel your bathroom, will it pay for itself when you put the house on the market next year? Given that your wife and you are real smart, what are the odds your kids will turn out to be at least as smart as you are? (A good thing to know before you push little Johnny and Mary to be doctors.)

If you've never read up on probability, don't worry, now that you know you have good reasons to learn it, you'll be interested, and being interested is the best and easiest way to learn anything.

9

TAKIN' CARE OF BUSINESS

Zach is visiting David at the Pine Valley jail. What's that about? Zach hates David. They trade insults, and then Zach informs David he has discovered the missing video that caught David drugging Adam and shipping him across the ocean. What a shocker!

"I've already shown it to the D.A.," Zach taunts. "You're history."

With a threatening stare, David growls, "They have to convict me first."

We feel a chill. Careful, Zach, we advise: Don't antagonize him. . . .

But is all this really any of our business?

Of course it is. Otherwise they wouldn't have broadcast

this episode of *All My Children* into millions of American homes.

What if it was happening next door instead of on TV? If we want to get in the middle of that, better bring the Kevlar.

Or we could mind our own business, thereby respecting another of life's little stop signs.

Ah, but what *is* our business? Of all the quandaries facing humans and cartoon characters on a daily basis, few are more complicated than deciding what is and is not our business. We're a curious species, and that's basically good. Without curiosity, we would have died out long ago because we had no idea how to make more of ourselves. In fact, curiosity is a central drive of almost everything with a brain. For a chance to look at an electric train running around a track, a monkey will learn and perform absurd tasks taught by silly humans in white coats. Similarly, for a dispensation to watch *Monday Night Football* in peace, men will rake the lawn, take out the garbage, and even attend the ballet with their wives and a vast audience of other women, who keep giving them and the scattering of other husbands and boyfriends in the audience amused little smiles.

While, on the whole, curiosity is a good thing, it can also be bad, like that time when you were a kid and you wanted to see if the wings you made out of two-by-fours and one of Mom's sheets would fly you from your roof to the neighborhood 7-Eleven.

Now, as then, curiosity about the wrong things can be downright dangerous.

For guidance on this finely nuanced subject of minding

our own business, we turn again to SpongeBob Square-
Pants. Patrick Star has just shown SpongeBob his "secret"
box. Sponge asks what's inside, and Patrick rightly points
out that if he tells, it won't be a secret anymore. This is
enough for SpongeBob. He respects Patrick's right to pri-
vacy and accepts that he doesn't have to know what is in that
box. They go on to something else, and the episode fizzles.

Not.

Say we're driving down the interstate on the way to an
important meeting. We're making good time, gonna be
early, get a chance to straighten our tie and/or freshen our
lipstick. Suddenly, we come around a bend and slam on the
brakes, warned by an infinite regression of pulsing red brake
lights. For the next forty-five minutes, we inch forward,
fuming and sweating (though the AC's on full blast), feeling
our safety margin evaporate, fearing the meeting will start
without us, we'll lose the account, get fired, and then our
spouse will leave us, and we'll end up sleeping on a grate.

Finally, we see it, the reason for the forty-five-minute
backup. Not a spectacular flaming accident that wiped out
two of the four lanes of traffic, not a spaceship that landed
in the middle of the road with the aliens using their probes
on everyone. Just a dark blue and yellow ocher state police
cruiser, and a late-model Jaguar, one of those bottle-green
ones. The cop, whose Smokey hat is tilted downward at
nearly a right angle over his face, is trying to see under the
bill to write up a ticket, while his forty-something victim in
Dockers and a blue-and-white-striped shirt rubs at his Brad
Pitt hair looking like he just chugged a gallon of that stuff
they make you drink before colonoscopies. . . .

And how do we know all this?

Because we slow down just like everyone else and gape, even though we have been cursing the ten thousand cars ahead of us for doing the same thing.

Is this poor man's humiliation really any of our business? Does he appreciate being gawked at by millions of strangers while a cop lectures him on letting this ticket for two hundred and sixty bucks be a lesson to him? This poor sucker's predicament is not the business of passing drivers, just as whatever is in Patrick's box is none of SpongeBob's concern. But SpongeBob feels the pull of that box. It kills him that Patrick knows something he doesn't know. Why is mean old Patrick being so selfish? What would a little peek hurt? Are they best friends or aren't they?

Having mustered all the usual rationalizations in his defense, Sponge breaks into Patrick's rock late at night. Patrick wakes up and catches him as he is about to slip out with the box, and what happens next isn't pretty. If you think you don't have to worry about what a starfish would do if you meddled in its business, you're being too literal. Please try and take this nosiness thing more seriously.

After all, nosiness is how the human race got in trouble in the first place. The Book of Genesis tells us Eve was walking in the Garden of Eden, and this pretty snake says, "Hey, beautiful," and calls her over to its tree. Invites her to get smarter by eating the tree's fruit, to which God had already said, *"No way."* A paradox ensues. Having not yet eaten of the tree of knowledge, how can Eve be savvy enough to see through the snake's guile? But if she eats the fruit and it wises her up to what a crappy deal the snake was offering, it's too late. Which is why we cut our original mom some slack for letting her natural curiosity curse mankind throughout the ages with pain, death, disease and the invention of double knits to clothe our formerly unimpeachable nakedness.

In a suspiciously similar story, Pandora can't resist opening the box Epimetheus tells her is none of her business. Lots of nasty Furies rush out, afflicting mankind with all manner of ills. Again, a woman fails to rein in her nosiness, leading us to conclude that the writers of these stories were all men.

It's all a matter of judgment and sensitivity. If Patrick had wanted to show SpongeBob what was in his box, it would have been rude not to at least pretend to care. Because Patrick did not want to open the box, the opposite response was called for. It's simple—we merely put ourselves in the other person's (or fish's) place and ask ourselves if we'd like to receive what we're about to dish out. If some things are our business and no one else's, then it follows that other people will want the same from us, tedious though that may be. If you're out to cure the common cold or pass your history test or find out what your sweetheart wants for Valentine's Day, your curiosity is good and you should go full speed ahead.

If you want to know how much your mother-in-law weighs, or whether your buddy really got the good deal he claims on his SUV, or who was the first woman your boyfriend ever slept with years before he knew you existed, then it might be better to remember these words of Dorothy Parker:

"The cure for boredom is curiosity. There is no cure for curiosity."

10

GOING FOR BROKE

Another stop sign in life is knowing how to avoid overdoing something. This chapter and the next examine this little stop sign. SpongeBob SquarePants is a wonderful fellow with a remarkable, infectious laugh, a generous spirit and a kind word for everyone, but he does have a certain tendency to keep singing after the music has stopped.

Let's join SpongeBob at the Goo Lagoon. The citizens of Bikini Bottom don't let the fact that they are underwater stop them from having their very own beach, where volleyball, sunbathing, and ice cream stands add up to the good life. Sponge is with Sandy on this particular day, showing off and cracking jokes in an effort to impress her. It's working pretty well until strapping big Larry the Lobster saunters up and lures her away with him to lift weights. Pumping iron is not the strong suit of anyone with SpongeBob's pipe cleaner arms. After Larry has lifted huge barbells to the cheers of a crowd in nearby bleachers, SpongeBob tries to lift two marshmallows on a stick. He strains until his pants rip. Everyone laughs. Though embarrassed, SpongeBob is also pleased at how ripping his pants has catapulted him back to the center of attention. So pleased is he that he goes all over the beach, ripping his pants to get laughs.

Behavioral psychologists call this operant conditioning. These "Behaviorists" believe that just about everything humans do is the result of the rewards and punishments that result when we're doing things. In an attempt to prove this, a psychologist with the rather ominous name of Skinner trained rats and pigeons to press levers by giving them food whenever they did. Critics pointed out that rats and pigeons aren't people. What was Skinner to do? You can't just put human beings in big boxes and wait until it occurs to them to press a lever before letting a pizza slide down the chute. Those who'd never used a vending machine might starve, and there are rules about how long you can keep people in boxes without feeding them.

So Skinner told his critics to buzz off and stop being pests.

In a scarier version of this experiment, a microelectrode was implanted in the pleasure center of a rat's brain. At the other end was a lever. When the rat pressed the lever, he felt like he had gone to heaven and was surrounded by ten beautiful virgin rats, all of whom thought he was the greatest stud ever. Needless to say, this rat and his fellow subjects pressed the lever over and over again as fast as they could,

neglecting to eat, groom themselves, tell on each other, or do any of the other things rats normally do. They would have starved to death if the experimenters hadn't taken them off the lever.

Feeling good is nice, right? But even feeling good can be taken to extremes, as the rats demonstrate.

SpongeBob really liked getting those laughs. He was a comic sensation, until he toured the whole beach for the second and third time, ripping his pants and hearing the laughs peter out as his act began to go stale. Confused and alone, exiled from the warm approval every extrovert craves, SpongeBob had an epiphany about quitting when he was ahead and put it to music.

We all know people who stay at the party after everyone else has gone home, and we're serving them their fourth coffee and using the potholders to cover our yawns, and they're great folks, and we had fun with them, but now it's over, and they don't know it. Or the quarterback who was once the greatest but can no longer throw the ball more than ten yards, and so he sits on the bench and replaces the fans' and his own great memories of him with sad ones. Life abounds with examples of not knowing when to quit, from the old lady with too much perfume to the three-hour movie that should have been two. It's a good idea to check now and then to make sure we're not in that camp. Do people's eyes glaze over when you say, "Stop me if I've told you this before"? Do they put little pieces of cotton in their ears when you start up another chorus of "Baby One More Time"? When you head for the water cooler to gossip with your coworkers, do you find them already there, falling strangely silent at your approach?

If so, realizing it is half the battle. Ease up, back off, learn to quit while you're ahead. Less can be more. Stop the sales pitch the minute they buy the shoes. Leave the party while they're still laughing at your jokes.

And, whatever you do, don't volunteer for an experiment where they tell you all you have to do is press a lever.

11

NO PAIN, NO PAIN

There's a lot of talk out there right now that the principal thing humans overdo is eating. So let's end our examination of stop signs with a word or two about how Bikini Bottom feels about dieting.

In SpongeBob's world, they hold a more relaxed attitude toward eating than the U.S. Department of Health and Human Services. Most characters in Bikini Bottom are fairly svelte (one hopes it is not because they eat a lot of fish). On the other hand, Mr. Krabs is a pear, Patrick is plump, and Mrs. Puff, the boating instructor, goes from zaftig to zeppelin when SpongeBob's driving miscues cause her to blow up. She is, after all, a puffer fish.

Bikini Bottom has no Department of Health and Fish Services to come out every five years with guidelines about what sea creatures should eat. Human dietary guidelines set forth by HHS in 2005 recommend two thousand calories a day and so many fruit and veggies that every household that follows the guidelines will need more toilets. It's nice that HHS is giving the control freaks of our society something to shoot for, but guess what—those folks are already thin.

Maybe the food feds got inspired by those experiments where rats lived a lot longer if you half starved them. Some scientists have concluded humans could do the same by drinking lots of water and eating only an occasional crust. This completely ignores the fact that the rats did not half starve themselves. They went along *because they were in cages and no one would let them have more food*. Doesn't that tell us something? Isn't it, in fact, the most significant undiscussed reality of the study?

The well-meaning folks at HHS haven't yet asked for funding to put the entire American public in cages and half starve them, but that's only because they are obviously in denial. Their own surveys show that one out of eight citizens followed the year 2000 dietary guidelines. So who had the bright idea of making them even stricter in 2005? Apparently, HHS doesn't get it that "one out of eight" is their report card. If the rest of us had gotten 13 percent on our tests in college we'd never have made it past freshman year.

High blood pressure, heart attack and the other health problems do appear to come more frequently to obese people. But life is full of trade-offs. Only you can decide whether the pleasure of eating more than you need is worth more to you than the health and other benefits of rationing.

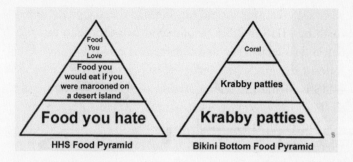

To all who think fat = stupid, or weak, or ugly, take care. We will more surely be damned for bigotry than bigness.

Whatever you decide in your own approach to meals, the next time someone quotes the new HHS food pyramid to you, you will be within your rights to quote the Bible back to them, Ecclesiastes 8:15: "A man hath no better thing under the sun than to eat, and to drink, and to be merry."

THE 3RD WAY

HARD TRUTHS

12

SHRTCTS

If there's anything humans and cartoon characters love more than getting what we want, it's getting it faster. One way to do this is to work harder.

So, naturally, we look for other ways.

This does not necessarily mean we are lazy, but simply that we feel a need to ration our energy. In our defense, paleoanthropologists suggest our preference for the elevator over the stairs comes from an instinct going back to our cave-dwelling days. Back then, finding enough food to go on finding enough food was all we thought about. There was no TV to watch, no Internet to cruise, and very little sitting around of any kind. No one worried that their buns were too big or their abs too small. Pedaling on a stationary bike would have made you the clan lunatic. Riverdance was when a saber-toothed tiger chased you into the water.

The saber-tooths are long gone, but we are still saving our energy. We avoid needless effort. Our genes have a jones for the quick fix.

And, yeah, some of us *are* lazy.

That's why there are shortcuts.

Tempting as the concept is, one of the hard truths mined for laughs in several *SpongeBob* episodes is that there are no shortcuts.

Merriam-Webster's two definitions of the word may help explain why:

1. A route more direct than the one ordinarily taken.
2. A method or means of doing something more directly and quickly than and often not so thoroughly as by ordinary procedure (a *shortcut* to success).

Question: If we know there's a route more direct than the one ordinarily taken, why don't we ordinarily take it? How many times must we take a shortcut before it *becomes* the ordinary route?

Yes, and how many roads must a man walk down before you call him a man?

When Squidward wanders around for days in the coral fields outside Bikini Bottom trying to deliver a pizza, we can say it's because he's lost. But surely there's more to it, or he'd listen when SpongeBob reads the moss on the rocks and tries to show him the way.

Maybe it's not that there are no shortcuts, but rather that we're no good at finding them.

History's most dramatic case of the long way around has to be Moses, an otherwise impressive person who took forty years to lead the children of Israel from Egypt to the promised land—four hundred miles as the crow flies. Granted, Humvees didn't exist in 1442 B.C., and you couldn't stop at a gas station to ask directions. But still. Four hundred miles over forty years works out to a bit over a thousandth of a mile per hour. Six feet. A tall person can get that far just by falling down. Moses wrote the best seller Exodus in part to justify his dismal navigating: God's will, folks. Moses wasn't lost, no way.

And even if he'd spotted a gas station, guys don't ask directions.

One day at the Krusty Krab diner, Mr. Krabs decides that, to boost morale, the employees should make gifts for each other, something that takes thought and effort. Welcoming this challenge with his usual zeal, SpongeBob knits a sweater from his own eyelashes for Squidward. For his part, Squid is so narcissistic he doesn't even remember he was supposed to make Sponge a gift. Fuming at the inconvenience, Squid hurries out and finds what he thinks is a pie vendor. Perfect! He can buy a homemade-looking pie for SpongeBob and claim he made it himself.

Squidward takes a shortcut.

At first glance, it looks like this quick fix should work, but that wouldn't be funny. Funny would be the pie containing a time bomb that will go off when it reaches SpongeBob's lower intestine, around sunset. (The idea for this episode seems to have come from the writer eating an overly spicy meatball the day before the script was due.)

When Squidward learns about the bomb and tries to get the pie back, he's too late. He only wanted to fake baking a pie for SpongeBob, and now he's sealed the little guy's doom. Wracked with guilt, Squid decides he must make the unsuspecting Sponge's final hours as wonderful as possible. This will take every minute of the rest of the day.

Squidward's shortcut has become a long haul.

But that's not the only problem with a shortcut—that it might not work. The other problem is that you'll never know what you missed by taking it. Every shortcut, whether it seems to work or not, creates a question: What would have happened if we'd rejected the shortcut and done the thing in full?

Remember that poem by Robert Frost they made us read in high school, "The Road Not Taken"? If you were a guy with some animal cunning, maybe you risked the scorn of your jock buddies to read "The Road Not Taken" aloud in class in a soulful voice, so Mary Jane St. Clair, the most beautiful girl at Central High, could see you with new eyes, realize how sensitive you are, and then agree to go to the drive-in to see *King Kong* with you—which you assured Mary Jane is a very poetic movie, even though Kong didn't know iambic meter from a blond meter maid.

If you didn't read the poem to the class, forget it, it's too late. Call it your road not taken.

Let's look at the road Squidward didn't take—baking a pie for SpongeBob. Never mind that if he'd done the work himself he'd have been confident there wasn't a bomb in the pie. That's probably not much of a risk outside of cartoons. Squidward took the shortcut because he didn't want to put himself out. Is there a reason we can offer that might make him *want* to put himself out? If he'd felt more warmly toward SpongeBob, that would make him want to bake the pie. Squidward certainly knows the little guy adores him. And some of his own feelings are revealed when Squidward realizes his shortcut is going to blow SpongeBob into a million mini sponges. Squid is so remorseful he spends the whole rest of the day trying to make the little guy happy. This proves he harbors some warm feelings for SpongeBob, too. It's just hard for Squidward to express warmth to anyone.

And that, right there, is a good reason for him to bake the pie.

In the next chapter we'll take a look at a revolutionary, life-changing concept research scientists in their nifty white coats have discovered in lab experiments about feeling and acting. This concept, if applied regularly, could lead to the kind of happiness Squidward missed out on when he faked that pie.

13

OUTSIDE THE BOX

Recall how B. F. Skinner spent his life telling anyone who would listen that people are basically big hairless rats who wear clothes? Well, other behavioral scientists took umbrage. "People have bigger brains than rats," these other theorists protested. "We humans think about things and stuff."

To sum up the anti-Skinner position: reward rocks, it is true, and punishment sucks, but we do more than just respond to carrots and sticks like a bunch of dumb old rats. For example, unlike rats, we can figure out that the guy in the lab coat who put us in the box wants us to press that lever. We can then refuse from pure spite.

In other words, we humans aren't just reflexes in bags of skin; we got *attitude*.

After loads of research to see how our attitudes affect what we do, it occurred to a couple of bright, outside-the-box thinkers to reverse the question: How might what we do affect our attitudes? Leon Festinger and James Carlsmith, psychologists both, rounded up seventy-one male college psych majors and gave them really boring tasks to do. One task was putting a bunch of spools on pegs on a tray, then taking them off again, using only one hand, and keeping it up for half an hour. When the subjects began to dislocate their jaws yawning, they were allowed to switch to another task—turning little pegs counterclockwise a quarter of a turn, using only one hand, then turning them back, and so on and so on.

If time is slipping away too fast for you, try spending it this way.

Afterward, Leon and James gave some of the guys a dollar to tell a young woman posing as a new subject for the same experiment that the study had been ever so much fun and really exciting. Leon and James gave another set of the test subjects twenty bucks to do the same thing. The rest of the subjects (the control group) weren't asked to tell anyone how exciting the experiment was. (If you're ever in an experiment that involves electricity and rubber truncheons, insist on being in the control group.)

At the end, Leon and Jimmy asked all the subjects how interesting they thought the tasks in the experiment were. "Boring," said the control group. "Boring," said the guys who'd been paid decent money to lie. "Uh, pretty interesting," said the guys who'd been given only a dollar to hype the study.

Then the study was over, and Leon and Jimbo took all the money back. (True!)

In a nutshell, here's what the experiment means: The control group, as expected, said "boring" because no one had messed with their heads. The guys who got a big reward (until the experimenters took it back) were able to tell themselves they lied for the cash, which left their real attitude toward the boring tasks unchanged. But the guys who were paid only a dollar had a problem: Leon and Jim had designed the experiment to set their brains ajangle with conflicting implications. They either had to believe they'd sold out for chump change or persuade themselves that doing all that dumb stuff had been interesting. This dilemma didn't necessarily occur to them in so many words; all they knew for sure was that their brains were jangling. Leon and James theorized that this test group, to get rid of the jangling, had let their own efforts to assure the young woman the study was interesting persuade them that they really did believe it was interesting.

Their behavior changed their attitude.

Leon and James then coined a name for what caused these poor, manipulated college boys to change their minds. They called it cognitive dissonance, because that term has six syllables, whereas "brain jangle" has only three. That night, the two experimenters went to Johnny Rockets to celebrate. As they left the table, they palmed the tip they'd left the waitress. (Joke.)

Mr. Krabs didn't offer Squidward twenty bucks to make Sponge a personal gift, or threaten to give him wedgies if he didn't. Squidward was so undermotivated that he plain forgot to bring a gift. When Krabs chided him, Squid went for the shortcut. If, instead, he had taken himself in hand and made the pie from scratch, he might well have decided that, hey, if he was going to all that trouble for SpongeBob, maybe he liked the little pest more than he thought. He'd have found a way to get across the feelings it was difficult for him to express, but that he needed to say for his own good.

Psychologist Albert Bandura describes the effects of behavior on attitude this way in his book *Principles of Behavior Modification*: "Those who behave contrary to their private opinions under conditions of minimal external inducement are obliged to discover new attractions in the disagreeable activity to justify to themselves their voluntary performance of inconsistent actions." If Bandura had written his book in English rather than Profbabble, this statement would have landed on page 108 instead of 608, but never mind that. The important point is that it can be easier to act yourself into a new way of feeling than to feel yourself into a new way of acting.

So whether your route to happiness is baking for your coworkers or building a better relationship with your boss, your spouse, or your pet chinchilla, don't fall into Squidward's shortcut trap. Acting the way you'd like to feel will probably work a lot better than waiting until you feel like acting that way.

A final note on shortcuts: If you're thinking of skipping ahead in this book, you'll miss how partying with Sponge and Patrick almost lands Mr. Krabs in therapy, what Squidward does when his life hits bottom, and why it can be good to stink.

14

DOG EAT DOG
WON'T HUNT

Another hard truth in life and *SpongeBob* episodes is that we can't just walk over other people to get what we want. Put it that way, and most people will agree. They'll tell you that a dog-eat-dog attitude is a bad thing, too nasty and aggressive.

Words to live by, politically correct to be sure, but how sincere are they? If we're so down on aggression, how come we cherish all those pithy quotations about winning at any cost?

One of our favorites is Leo Durocher's, "Nice guys finish last." Durocher was a baseball star back when ballplayers wore uniforms rough as tree bark, never rubbed where the fastball drilled them, and went out of their way to slide into each other's shinbones with steel claws on the tips of their shoes. So when Leo said "Nice guys finish last," it was widely assumed he meant last in the baseball standings. What many people don't realize or have forgotten is, such a loverboy was Leo that a beautiful actress left her husband to marry him.

This beautiful actress called him "Lippy."

Uh-huh, uh-huh.

But let's say, for the sake of argument, that Leo really did mean last in the standings. Let's even assume he was right. (Never mind nice-guy winners like Mickey Mantle, Al Kaline and Lou Gehrig.) If we have to be jerks to finish first, is it worth it?

SpongeBob and Squidward face this decision together when it comes time, once again, for Mr. Krabs to name the Employee of the Month. Up to this point, nice-guy SpongeBob has won this contest every single month with such monotonous regularity that identical pictures of his face, grinning with pride, cover an entire wall of the Krusty Krab (a spooky wall, in that it shimmers into being only for this episode and is gone in the next episode as if it never existed). When Sponge asks Squid if he's gonna try to win the Employee of the Month prize this time, Squidward snidely informs him that the "contest" is just a cynical ruse by Mr. Krabs to motivate a certain gullible employee to work harder, longer, and for less money.

This strikes at the heart of SpongeBob's self-image. He suggests Squidward is jealous because he can't win. Squid sputters at this gut-shot to his own deepest conceit—that he is superior in all things. In seconds, Squid goes from scorn to a feverish will to win the contest at any cost.

The stage is set for dog eat dog.

Note that the trigger for this is anger. Sponge and Squid rile each other up and then turn aggressive. A large part of the charm of Bikini Bottom is that it's a mellow place, normally. SpongeBob might be a yellow cube of pure energy, but he's rarely aggressive. Squidward is easily irritated, but he's not really aggressive either. He just wants to be left alone. Mr. Krabs can get cranky about losing money, but on the whole, he maintains his piratical cheer.

The only character in Bikini Bottom whose normal state is aggression is Plankton, Mr. Krabs's tiny, belligerent rival for Bikini Bottom's restaurant trade. Plankton continually uses and abuses SpongeBob in an effort to steal the recipe for Krabby Patties so his Chum Bucket restaurant can outdraw the Krusty Krab. Even so, SpongeBob refuses to get angry with him. He feels Plankton is misunderstood, and if he only had a friend, he'd be all right. That Sponge-Bob is wrong about this is not Sponge's loss but Plankton's. Perpetually angry and discontent, pumped up on his endless supply of indignation, the competitive midge Plankton lives a life of misery, failure and loneliness. His only real accomplishment is to provide the contrast that magnifies Sponge-Bob's kindness.

This makes SpongeBob's and Squidward's aggressive tactics in the Employee of the Month contest all the more startling. In the heat of this struggle, the normally sunny SpongeBob tries to bury Squidward, then ties him to a wrecked ship to keep him from getting to work. Once Squidward's competitive fire is lit, the normally blasé cephalopod is willing to cut SpongeBob into little rectangular pieces to win.

Dog-eat-dog aggression like this, while rare in Bikini Bottom, may be seen at any time of day on most channels on your TV dial. (Note: If your set has an actual dial, it's time to buy a new TV. They have color now!) "Reality TV" contestants put everything on the line to win; the losers are hollowed out into teary, blubbering shells of their former selves. *Crossfire*, as the title suggests, gets people together for the sole purpose of goading them to fight.

Turn off your set and step out into the world, and you'll see it there, too. A big chain store moves into your neighborhood and undersells Pete's Hardware until it is dead, dead, dead. Airlines bankrupt themselves in their frenzy to put each other out of business. Politicians do and say anything to get elected, then wonder why we think they're scum.

While it might seem all the rage now, the truth is, dog eat dog has been around since the Precambrian epoch, six hundred million years ago, when the first cells had to beat each other to the nutrients they needed to live. Later, cavemen wiped out the saber-toothed tiger to survive. Later still, our ancestors, feeling threatened by the Neanderthals, eradicated them from the face of the earth.

That was then. Now we have a nice counterweight called civilization, which the human and cartoon races have worked very hard to build so they won't have to shoot their coworker dead in the morning because there is only one cup left in the Mr. Coffee. Civilization may someday decline, but thankfully we have not yet reached the state of overpopulation where, to assure a continuing food supply, we'll need to bring the Soylent Green. (This is not a color in the

Homeland Security spectrum; it's the hue people in the movie of the same name turn when they finally wise up that the food pellets they are eating aren't Spam.)

Most of us want civilization to work. Aside from a few mutant killers out there, we all pretty much believe in it. So why is it so easy to blow off how far we've come in a split second and go back to all-out warfare over things like being cut off in traffic, or someone else's ugly, talentless brat beating out our beautiful little darling for the cheerleading team?

The next and final chapter of The Third Way will spotlight Albert Bandura's "landmark" experiment on aggression, then discuss why SpongeBob and Squidward and too many other good citizens find it so easy to go after each other. The Third Way will conclude with a SpongeBobian solution for lowering our own temperatures when those superheated moments come along.

15

VALLEY OF THE BOBO DOLLS

No less a legend than the great Vince Lombardi, head coach of the Green Bay Packers (back when their fans didn't wear cheese hats), is said to have proclaimed: "Winning isn't everything; it's the only thing."

Another of our cherished aphorisms about the joys of aggression.

But take heart, gentle readers. Vince Lombardi didn't say that. John Wayne said it in the 1953 movie *Trouble Along the Way*. John Wayne looked, sounded, and walked tough, our national hero with fused hips and gravel in his throat, but we must remember his job was acting. The line did not come from John Wayne's hard-won lessons in life, but from a clever screenwriter who probably weighed a hundred and forty pounds soaking wet.

In our heart of hearts we all know that destroying a village doesn't save it. It is the heat of the moment that sweeps up SpongeBob and Squidward in such a powerful lust for victory at any cost that they trash the Krusty Krab in an orgy of mindless aggression, destroying the very institution that was to give one of them the Employee of the Month award.

Psychologists have been looking at aggression for a long time, trying to figure out where it comes from. One of the most famous studies was done by Albert Bandura, whose book we quoted from earlier. Big Al suspected the reason we lapse into acts of violence is because we have seen other people do it. To test this hypothesis, he persuaded the parents of seventy-two children between the ages of three and six to loan their little sweeties to him for an experiment. Half the children were girls and half boys. Dr. Bandura hired a male and female assistant to help him with the experiment. (And actually let them keep the money!) The experiment had three phases. In the first, small subgroups of the children were brought into a playroom and given some nonaggressive toys to enjoy. One of the adult assistants (called models) also came into the room and did one of two things. The model either played quietly with Tinkertoys or began to attack a Bobo doll that was in the room.

Bobo, for those of you born after 1961, was an inflatable clown with a big, weighted bottom. You could punch Bobo over and over, and he would always pop back up. When the models attacked Bobo, they also berated it, shouting, "Pow! Sock him in the nose!" and similar trash talk.

Next the kids were taken to a second room and annoyed by the experimenter. This was done by showing them neat toys, then telling them they couldn't play with them.

Third, each group of boys and girls was taken into yet another room in Bandura's labyrinth and given other toys to play with, including a Bobo doll and mallet, and also dart guns.

Does anyone doubt that the little urchins who had seen the models hammering on Bobo and bad-mouthing the poor defenseless doll did the same thing? The boys who'd watched a male adult hammer did more hammering of their own than boys who had seen the man playing with Tinker-toys. Interestingly, little girls who watched a woman hammer on the doll showed some confusion, saying things like, "She's a lady, she's not supposed to act like that."

Men, let us all hang our heads in a moment of shame at our inferior natures.

Okay, enough. Getting back to Bandura, important as his experiment is said to be, it would be unfair to blame all subsequent violence in the world on him and his associates. After all, only seventy-two children were shown by adults that punching and kicking and trash-talking are acceptable.

The Bobo doll experiment has been used to condemn violence on TV, but those who use it this way forget to explain why, if TV has such power to take over our brains, the overwhelming majority of kids who watch violent TV never go out and copy what they see. It's really hard to tell for sure if violent TV or movies make people more violent, or if people who like to watch such stuff are drawn to it because they are already more violent.

Aggression does seem to be much more common in males. Researchers have spent a lot of time measuring the amount of the male hormone testosterone in various bad-boy men compared to their Mister Rogers counterparts. Turns out nice guys have as much testosterone as the bad boys. As noted in chapter 1, little boys learn at an early age that they mustn't show fear and that it is not all right to cry. What does that leave? Scare a man and he gets angry. Make a man sad and he gets angry.

Hmmmm.

For a final quote on aggression, we turn to Jean-Paul Sartre, who said: "Once you hear the details of a victory, it is hard to distinguish it from a defeat."

True, Sartre was part of that country that recently caused some of us to pour our Châteauneuf du Pape down the drain. But, unlike John-Wayne, Jean-Paul at least played some pro football. . . .

Or was that Romain Sartre?

Never mind. We really don't need quotes from famous people to get what aggression is all about. Instead, next time we feel like grinding someone's nose in the ground, we might try taking a time-out to go watch our DVDs of *SpongeBob SquarePants* in all those episodes where he is not filled with maniacal zeal to win Employee of the Month. Your blood pressure will go down. You will smile. In the eleven minutes it takes to watch Sponge's niceness and goodness carry him through all his many trials, the neuro-chemicals of aggression that flood your system when you get mad will have time to drain out before you put someone else's or your own head through a wall. You will feel better.

If you feel angry a lot, maybe it would also be good to find a time and place to let yourself feel the fear or sadness beneath. Go off by yourself and tell it like it is. Make up a little ballad, maybe, like Sponge did after he saw the error of ripping his pants to get attention. The ballad can be about you being scared. Or sad. If you feel tears coming, don't clench your jaw until your teeth crack, just go ahead and cry. Seriously. No one will know. If you started out a man, you'll still be a man after you "get that piece of grit out of your eye," and you might be a better one. You might even rent one of those movies you always avoid because they make you want to cry. Watch it alone, and let the floodgates open, because tears actually carry neurochemicals of sadness out of our bodies, like blowing the rust out of pipes.

And if you're married to someone wise, or have a true

friend in life, you might let that person in on how you're feeling, too—not the anger, which is the symptom, but the underlying sickness of fear or sadness beneath. At the very least, it beats yelling, or worse, taking a swing at your boss or that waiter who sneered at you for drinking red wine with fish. And if you try to cry and you just can't do it, and the very thought of confiding renders you mute, by all means, get yourself a Bobo doll and a hammer.

Just make sure the kids aren't watching.

THE 4TH
WAY

ECONOMICS

16

NO FREE LUNCH

The economics of a happier life get plenty of play in Bikini Bottom. In one episode, SpongeBob invents a new concept for Krabby Patties that draws nothing but scorn from the uninventive Mr. Krabs and Squidward. The little yellow guy must then believe in himself enough to test his colorful idea in the local economy. In another episode, Mr. Krabs's penny-pinching—of a dime in this case—expands into a life crisis for Squidward that will sorely test the patience of Sponge-Bob. In yet another episode, which we'll examine in a later chapter, we witness the dire consequences of shoplifting a balloon.

The founding principle of the Krusty Krab is "No Free Lunch." Owner Eugene Krabs has been known to offer his patrons free water, but that is like a McDonald's manager throwing in free air with a Big Mac. SpongeBob and Patrick get into trouble not with free lunches but with free rides. It begins when Patrick discovers these interesting hooks on the ends of lines that dangle down from on high. When he gives one of these hooks an experimental jerk, it swoops away toward the surface. Patrick, who is a nut for games of any kind, quickly realizes he can seat himself in the comfy curve of these hooks and take off on a thrillingly fast ride far above Bikini Bottom, *absolutely free of charge*! As he nears the surface, he lets go and drifts back down, trunks ballooning, for a soft landing. Patrick can't imagine any possible danger in what he's doing.

We of the race of fishermen know better, of course.

Given that humans invented the "no free lunch" saying, why is it that thirty-four million Americans get scammed out of forty billion dollars a year by telemarketers alone?

Clearly, we *do* believe in free lunches. The reason can be

summed up in one word: childhood. By the time we leave our teens, we've formed a huge percentage of our lifelong beliefs. Parents, teachers, preachers, siblings and playground pals fill our heads with the way things should be. If all goes well, most of this learning is useful, like not eating dirt or bitch-slapping your football coach. However, some of what we learn can mess with our heads, which is why shrinks keep pushing us for details of our childhoods. It isn't just because they are nosy and obsessed. It's because shrinks know that much of what we believe—the illogical and harmful along with the good—we learned so long ago that we have now forgotten we learned it, and therefore are unlikely to challenge the haywire life scripts of any of these screwy beliefs on our own.

"Free lunch" is one of the best hidden and most tenacious of these false beliefs. By the age of two, we've bought into it totally, because our whole life up to that point has been nothing but free lunches. Alas, Sigmund Freud himself couldn't get us to remember doing this, because everything before that third candle on our cake is pretty much a blank.

To be honest, for some of us, the free lunches continued all the way up to when our parents informed us they were not going to pay for a sixth year of college in which we continued to party down, sleep until noon, and cut all the boring classes, while promising to get our degree next year, for sure. This shocking derailment of the gravy train brought to a close an astonishing era of free goodies—not just lunch, but breakfast and dinner, clothes, housing, heat in the winter and AC in the summer, vacations, toys at holidays and birthdays, use of the car for our senior prom—in short, just about everything we thought of as rightfully ours, even though we never paid a cent for it nor did anything in particular to deserve it.

Small wonder that, in our heart of hearts, we're still hoping for a free lunch.

If you think you're an exception to this, you're probably defining "free lunch" too narrowly, like an actual lunch that is free, or any other business transaction where we try to get something for nothing. The figures on such rip-off schemes are bad enough, amounting to billions of dollars fleeced from Americans every year. The Web site of the U.S. Secret Service keeps us up to date on the latest scams. The sober agents with the silvered sunglasses, polite to a fault, have posted this warning:

> Unfortunately, there is a perception that no one is prone to enter into such an obviously suspicious relationship. However, a large number of victims are enticed into believing they have been singled out from the masses to share in multimillion dollar windfall profits for doing absolutely nothing.

Translation: "Don't think you can't be this stupid."

But we do, don't we. Ha-ha. We don't get taken. Not us, just people like us.

So Patrick is playing with the hooks, oblivious to the danger. On his way to work, SpongeBob passes by and Patrick persuades him to take a few "free" rides himself. Then Sponge's sense of responsibility kicks in and he continues on to work, where Mr. Krabs, wise in the ways of fishing poles, warns him never to mess with the hooks. SpongeBob ignores Mr. Krabs's warning, and we get to see what happens when someone else (not us) thinks they can get a free lunch, or in this case, launch.

Maybe none of us are so dim we'd respond to a letter from "a Nigerian government official" informing us that he is seeking a reputable foreign company or individual into whose account he can deposit funds ranging from $10 million to $60 million that the Nigerian government overpaid on some procurement contract. But what about those "buy one, get one free" offers you see in grocery stores? All the sign has to say is "three for six dollars," and we'll buy the three, even though it's jars of those little pearl onions you put in Gibsons, and you drink one Gibson per year on New Year's Eve, and one-third of three jars (which would last you until 2084) is priced at exactly one-third of six dollars.

And what about raking your lawn to save the fifty bucks you'd have to pay the skinny neighbor kid with the baggy low-rise jeans and triple-X sweatshirt? Let's say it takes you five hours to get the leaves into piles, rake them onto the tarp, and lug them down to the street. After the first bracing half hour, during every remaining minute you'd rather be inside where it's warm doing almost anything else. Your shoulder will be sore for a week, but by cracky you got rid of those pesky leaves for free . . . if you ignore the fact that, when you go in to work on Monday, you'll be making twenty-five dollars an hour, which means you could have traded five hours of hard physical work, a sore shoulder, and a flare-up of your leaf mold allergy for two comfy hours at your desk.

Raking your own leaves is not free.

But when all is said and done, buying onions on sale or doing yardwork so you won't have to "pay" for it are small potatoes. The "free lunch" scam that costs us the most in life has nothing to do with money.

17

LOVE IS A LUNCH

The lunch many of us keep trying to eat for free is love.

Wait, you protest. Love *is* free. There's a word for people who charge for love. Yes, there is, and the word has two letters, but it's not "ho."

The word is "us."

Love is the number-one human transaction where people who wouldn't fall for any other setup scam themselves into expecting a free lunch.

This is exactly what Patrick does in one of the more openly satirical episodes of *SpongeBob*. Sponge and Pat have found an orphaned baby clam and decide to make a game of raising it. SpongeBob takes on the duties of mothering the clam while Patrick goes off to "work." What starts out as a fun game for both pals stays a fun game for Patrick, whose "job" consists of loafing around and watching TV all day. He comes home "too tired" to give SpongeBob any help with baby clam. He watches more TV instead while Sponge buds extra arms so he can simultaneously iron, change diapers, feed the baby its bottle and so on. Sponge soon becomes exhausted and resentful. Patrick remains oblivious.

Hard to imagine where the creators of SpongeBob got the idea for this episode.

The blunders we make because we expect love to be free would surely add up to the number-one cause of divorce. Talking honestly about the quid pro quo in love seems antiromantic and crass, so we don't. Instead, we cling to the self-serving illusion that folks should love us for what we "are." The danger in this, to paraphrase a recent U.S. president, is that it depends on what your definition of "are" is.

There are two ways to define people. The first is by what they are. The second is by what they do. For ourselves, we instinctively use the first definition. For example, "I am a stud." For others, we use the second. For example, "He couldn't get a date if he were the last man on Earth."

Notice that the second definition tells us a lot more than the first. That's because it's about specific behavior rather than a generalized notion of inner qualities. Thinking of ourselves in terms of who or what we "are" is dangerous to relationships because, too often, our concept of our inner selves doesn't match up very well with what others see us do (or not do).

Example: If you want to know how charitable people are, you can make it a question on a survey: "How charitable are you on a scale of one to ten?" Most people asked this question will score themselves fairly high, lots of sevens and eights and some nines and tens, with an average score well above five.

Suppose, instead, you ask this question: "How often do you donate money or time to charitable causes? Once a week? Once a month? Every few months? Once a year?" Whenever social psychologists do surveys like this they get significantly different results between "are" and "do." Even in the months after the heartbreaking tsunami of December 2004, the number of people who considered themselves charitable would be much greater than the number of people who report actually giving money to charities. When we are allowed to characterize ourselves, we come out *much* better than on the Piggly Wiggly security videotape that shows us scarfing a Zagnut that never makes it to checkout. People will believe they are affectionate when in actual life they hug their significant others less often than they change their furnace filters. Then they wonder why they're out in the cold.

Question: Where did we get the idea we shouldn't have to do anything to be loved?

A. From Britney Spears's autobiography.

B. From the back of a Wheaties box.

C. From childhood.

The correct answer is C. Once again, it is those crucial early experiences that set us up to believe that we should be loved for what we are. Those of us with reasonably good and decent parents felt at least some love from day one, long before we did anything to deserve it. It was all too easy to learn the wrong lesson from this—that love, like so much else in our lives at that time, is free and we don't have to do a thing to earn it and that, as an adult, we will continue to have love lavished on us just for being us.

In the first place, it isn't really true that your parents loved you just for being you. That sounds nice, but the unsentimental truth is that you weren't that different in how you looked or acted from any other newborn of your sex and race with ten fingers and toes. If a myopic nurse had switched you on day one with another baby, your parents would have loved you just as much, so long as they didn't know you weren't "theirs."

You were loved because you were a small bundle of life in which Mom saw her eyes and Dad his hands and smile. You were the product of their physical love and a sweet reminder of it. You were the focus of a lot of their hopes and dreams. They gazed into your crib and thought about the day you'd be a caring doctor, with a white coat and a stethoscope, or a fine district attorney in a nice suit defending society from depraved criminals. (Note that your parents did not imagine you using your law degree to sue the doctor, nor did they envision their doctor version of you amputating a healthy leg because you missed the words "Take this one" the surgical nurse scrawled in huge magic marker letters on the sick leg.) We experienced free love when we were babies, so now we believe we ought to be loved simply because we're us.

We need to *grow up*.

The reason it is *impossible* to be loved for yourself is that no one around you has any direct way of knowing what that "self" is. No one can crawl inside your skin and experience what is going on in your heart. It seems obvious, but we ignore this all the time. Feeling love for someone is very nice—for you. All anyone else knows about your feelings is what you show them. That warm fuzzy feeling you have for them won't count for anything if you don't act on it to make them feel it, too.

Dr. Lora Lovehandles, noted authority on marriage (and Ph.D. in medieval French), has devised this simple test that you can take in forty-five seconds to tell what kind of life partner you are. There are only two questions. Ready? Compare these two statements: (A) "It's your turn to load the dishwasher." (B) "It's my turn to load the dishwasher."

Question 1: Which would you rather hear from your significant other?

Question 2: Which would you rather say to your significant other?

If you answered (B) to both questions 1 and 2, you are a good significant other.

If you answered (A) to question 1 and (B) to question 2, you are either a saint or a liar.

If you answered (B) to question 1 and (A) to question 2, you are not only a bad significant other, you know nothing about taking tests.

SpongeBob and Patrick modeled their partnership in raising the baby clam along the lines of a stereotypical traditional marriage. We'd have a lot more sympathy for Patrick's case if he'd had a job other than eating ice cream. Traditional marriages can work for the right two people, just as they'd be a disaster for the wrong two. What matters is not what role a given party plays but what is fair. The paradox of wanting nothing more than to flop back in an easy chair and let someone else clean up the dishes is that if you do this a lot, you will not be able to shrug off the guilt you know, deep down, is warranted. You will not feel right with yourself, and the chair won't feel all that good—unless you're a psychopath, in which case there's no talking to you anyway, so go flop in the chair and leave the rest of us alone.

The bottom line is to stop thinking of yourself in terms of what you are and hold yourself to the standard by which others are obliged to judge you—what you do. Putting a smile on the face of your partner or friend or spouse takes only a few minutes and is the quickest, easiest way to get the same back at you.

Expect love to be free, and sooner or later life will hand you your lunch.

18

i OF THE BEHOLDER

The artful giving of gifts is an indispensable part of the economics of happiness in Bikini Bottom and our own world. Let's see if we can sponge off the confusion that clouds our minds when it's time to buy that "perfect" present for someone.

SpongeBob loves to go jellyfishing. (If this seems to have no connection to gifts, wait for it.) Sponge can think of no finer way to spend a day than to grab his net, put on his "Big Bopper" glasses, and head off to the jellyfish fields with pal Patrick. One day, on their way to the fields, they happen upon Squidward and ask him along. For Squidward the introvert, grabbing a net and chasing through fields of seaweed trying to capture a jellyfish that can sting like an electric eel is entirely too real.

He could politely say, "No, thank you, boys. I know you enjoy jellyfishing and that's very nice, but I prefer other activities, such as sitting quietly alone in my giant stone-idol-shaped home, fuming."

Instead, he mockingly assures them there's nothing in this world he'd rather do than drop everything else and go jellyfishing with them. That his voice drips with sarcasm is lost on the literal sponge and starfish. Their joy turns to incomprehension as Squid pedals off without them on his bike. Chortling at his own sarcasm, Squidward will have no one but himself to blame, for he will soon suffer one of the oldest forms of human "generosity"—being given the gift the giver would like to get.

"What's wrong with that?" some of you may ask. Give unto others what you would have them give unto you—hey, it's almost like the golden rule, right?

Wrong, and the best proof is the day after Christmas.

Surely one of the better-kept secrets in polite society is that people need lessons in gift giving. December 26 is when this sad truth is quietly swept under the rug for another year. Remember when SpongeBob knitted Squidward a sweater from his eyelashes? Squidward flung it back in his face, and Sponge cried so hard he was able, on the spot, to knit Squid a sweater of his tears. Sponge's hurt feelings that day struck a spark of guilt even in the self-centered Squidward. No decent person wants to hurt someone else's feelings, which is why we know we must be gracious when the sister we gave a cashmere sweater gives us groundhog slippers that make our feet look as big as Shaquille O'Neal's. It's just not polite to tell Aunt Addie that her gift of pickled lemons in the quaint replica of a Ball jar from the gourmet section of Nordstrom is too big to be a paperweight, too fragile to make a good doorstop, and not quite heavy enough to knock out burglars that might creep into the house.

So each year, in the days after Christmas, as many as one-third of us slink into stores to return unwanted gifts, hoping that the giver will not visit us any time soon to make sure we have replaced our nineteenth-century ormolu mantel clock with the plastic statue of Bart Simpson sporting a twenty-first-century Timex in its stomach. Over the course of a year, a hundred billion dollars' worth of merchandise is returned in America. It's starting to annoy merchants so much that they're installing software on their cash register computers that will track your return history. If you come back too often with Aunt Addie's pickled lemons or the tie that lights up and plays "Jingle Bells," the merchant is going to tell you tough luck.

Why all this dissatisfaction with gifts? Isn't it the thought that counts?

Clearly, there's often a big gap between what the giver and receiver think is a gift. We all know that if we don't like or want a gift given to us, it is forbidden to let the giver know we are dissatisfied with it. Some of you may be saying, "Unless it's from a family member, right?"

Wrong. The prohibition against rejecting a gift goes double for family members, where the hurt of this rejection, however it might be denied, is likely to be the most rancorous. No, if returns are to be made, they must be made quietly, with adequate safeguards against being found out.

That said, let's return to our obligation as givers of

gifts. The reason we do so is to please the receiver, so it is simply a natural law that only the receiver can decide if that has happened. If our beloved cousin Blanche must search all over town trying to find the store where she can return the soap with the Hilton "H" stamped into it, we have probably not pleased her.

The author's grandmother and great-aunt came up with a simple way to avoid sneaking around behind each other's backs returning presents. Every Christmas, each gave the other a crisp, new twenty-dollar bill. When the two sisters got older and both were living on Social Security, they decided that twenty dollars was too much. From then on, they exchanged ten-dollar bills.

While this solution is elegant and even has a certain demented logic, it is not recommended for the general public. A better solution is to try and put ourselves in the place of the one who will receive our gift. Just spend a little time imagining, based on what we know about the person, what he or she might like to receive as a gift. Does Uncle Joe Bob, whom we've never seen in a shirt with a collar, and whose idea of fun is a six-pack and the stock car races, really need that spiffy tie with Bach's face glowering out from it? Or might he like, say, tickets to NASCAR's Budweiser Shootout? If you don't know enough to answer such a question, why are you giving Uncle Joe Bob a gift in the first place?

Let's tune in on Squidward again. Chortling at his putdown of Patrick and SpongeBob's jellyfishing invitation, he fails to watch where he's going and ends up falling off a cliff and severely hurting himself. When Sponge and Pat find out he's laid up, they want to make him feel better. They decide they're going to give him a gift—the best day ever in his life. They show up at his house full of plans. Squid, wrapped mummylike from head to toe in bandages, cannot speak. He is confined to a wheelchair. So what do SpongeBob and Patrick decide to give him? Do they read to him from his favorite book? Get him a nice, soft easy chair that will take some of the pain out of his bruises? Offer to run errands for him?

No. They present him with what would mean the best day ever for them.

A day of jellyfishing.

The mute Squidward has no second chance to explain in all earnestness that he wouldn't want to go jellyfishing even if he weren't a helpless invalid confined to a wheelchair and unable even to grip the handle of the jellyfish net. He's stuck. His fate will be decided by generosity, SpongeBob- and Patrick-style.

Giving the wrong gift goes all the way back to Genesis, when Cain, the gardener of Eden, offered God fruit and vegetables. His brother Abel offered the Big Guy the best of his flock of sheep and some "fat thereof." Apparently God was on the Atkins diet at the time, because He liked Abel's meat and fat and sent Cain's fruit basket back to the return counter. Cain got so mad over this rejection that he killed Abel.

The troublemakers among you are saying, "Why should we try to give the best gift if it just gets us killed?"

You are drawing the wrong lesson from this charming story. The right lesson is that if Cain had done some home- work, like checking with God's chef, he could have been sit- ting in Abel's living room a few years later, ruffling the hair of his nephews and nieces, instead of going around with God's mark on him, bringing forth fruit by the sweat of his brow.

While the consequences of giving the wrong gift are seldom so dire as being cast out of paradise and branded as the world's first murderer, giving the right gift is important all the same. It is one of the ways to happiness, because it enables us to reap the rewards of showing that we know a little something about someone, and that we care enough to give it some thought. Guys, if she's never set foot inside a hardware store, she doesn't really need a power drill for her birthday, right? And gals, you know that getting him silk underwear because that's what you'd like him to get you is iffy at best. If he's metrosexual, and you're sure about that, go for it. But if he channel surfs through *Queer Eye* without stopping and he always favored 100 percent cotton boxers, there's a reason.

The bottom line on gifts is that they are not a duty that comes with Christmas, Hanukkah, Kwanzaa and birthdays. They are an opportunity on those occasions, or no occasion at all, to show that you care about someone. You do not show this by getting them something you have no idea whether they will like. It is not "the thought" that counts. It's the gift. Especially when the recipient is someone you love. If you believe you love someone, and yet you don't know what to get her or him, it's one of nature's warning signs that you need to spend more time and mental effort putting yourself in the place of this loved one. What do they like? What do they dislike? What would mean a lot to them, coming from you? If you put yourself through this exercise on a regular basis, the benefits to the relationship will extend far beyond what you give each other for Valentine's or any other day.

THE 5TH WAY

WAY

TIMING

19

PROCRASTINATE LATER

The Fifth Way is about timing. The yin and yang of timing, illustrated in *SpongeBob* episodes, are the art of knowing when to quit and the perils of not starting (that is, procrastination). Chapters 19 and 20 will deal with the yang of procrastination, because it's the dark side of the two and we should deal with it first and not put it off.

Chapters 21 and 22 will explore the yin of knowing when to quit and cut our losses.

SpongeBob SquarePants is an on-time guy. He's never late to work. When he and Patrick take Mr. Krabs out on the town, Krabs suggests the two pick him up around 8:00. In his trademark "I'm cool" drawl, Sponge warns Krabs he'll be fashionably late—then shows up at 8:01. Throwing a big party for his Bikini Bottom friends, SpongeBob experiences profound fear of rejection when the time he printed on the invitations arrives and his doorbell has yet to ring (because his guests all know what "fashionably late" actually is).

One might say SpongeBob is obsessed with being on time.

So when Mrs. Puff, his Boating School instructor, assigns an eight-hundred-word essay on "What Not to Do at a Stoplight," the last thing on Sponge's mind is procrastination. He is as excited as the other students are bummed. He views the essay as a chance to bring himself one step closer to his ultimate goal in life: a driver's license.

Sponge is enthusiastic as he prepares to do the assignment. He tells himself this will be the best paper ever written on the subject. He starts early, laying the materials out on his desk, paper squared away, pencil sharpened. He writes the title: "What Not to Do at a Stoplight," and then his name: "by SpongeBob SquarePants. . . ."

And then he stalls.

As we can see from the illustration below, one out of five people in the general population has a serious procrastination problem.

Among college students, this number shoots all the way up to seven out of ten. The reason is obvious: professors. If they'd stop assigning homework and just let you sleep, all would be well.

A novel approach to handling the pressure of party-pooping profs can be drawn from the life of Winston Churchill, Britain's great wartime leader and lousy student. Faced with an exam on which he knew he would be asked for an in-depth analysis of one of thirty different countries,

Winnie put off studying until there was no possibility he could learn about all thirty countries in the time left before the test. He then wrote the name of each nation on a piece of paper and put them all in a derby hat, like in those old posters for *A Clockwork Orange*. He drew out one slip of paper and devoted his scant remaining time to cramming on that one country.

The nation he studied was on the test, and Winston wore derbies from then on.

This would be an excellent study technique for you if you are another Winston Churchill. Remember, he's the guy who said, "There is nothing quite so exhilarating as to be shot at and missed." Only a lucky man could say that. Winston was shot at and missed a *lot* fighting hand to hand against the Dervishes in 1898. Later, in the Boer War, he escaped a murderous ambush set just for him. For most of his adult life, Churchill smoked big cigars and drank more than a quart of cognac a day, and lived to be eighty-seven. If you think you have that kind of luck, by all means adopt his study techniques.

Seriously though, procrastination is a terrible thing and would be far easier to condemn were it not for all the famous people who set such bad examples. Churchill was not alone in being a historical eminence who procrastinated. Robert Benchley said, "Anyone can do any amount of work, provided it isn't the work he is supposed to be doing at that moment." And Mark Twain advised, "Never put off until tomorrow what you can put off until the day after tomorrow."

General George McClellan, commander of the Union Army of the Potomac at the beginning of the Civil War, polished procrastination to a high shine, drilling his men in marching and boot buffing and how to pitch a tent so tight a coin would bounce off the canvas. During one of the few battles he got sucked into, he noticed it was four o'clock, and so he brought out the pewter tea set he carried around with him and ordered crumpets for himself and his officers, apparently unaware they were all in a flop sweat. One of them nervously reminded McClellan about the Confederate attack coming at them that very moment on their right flank. McClellan's response was, "Patience, patience, we'll take care of it later." As the tea was being poured, the Confederate cavalry charged through his tent and sent the pewter teacups spinning.

McClellan lived to avoid fighting another day, but the cost to society of chronic procrastinators can be large. In the next chapter, we'll take a slightly more sober look at these costs, then reveal the secret weapons SpongeBob and the rest of us can use to put off procrastinating forever.

20

THE SALMON
OF DOUBT

We can understand a general being reluctant to lead his boys into a storm of hot lead. What was Leonardo da Vinci's excuse for taking twenty years to finish the *Mona Lisa*? Maybe it was because he couldn't decide if she was smiling or not. Some of you might not care that it took Leonardo so long to do a simple painting. Easy for you to say, now that we've had Mona around for five hundred years to tickle the art critics and mystify the mystery buffs. But what if it had taken John Lennon and Paul McCartney twenty years to write "Love Me Do"? Does anyone believe we'd ever have heard of the Beatles? We'd all have been the poorer, except maybe the No-see-'ums, that other group from Liverpool that was trying to start up at the same time.

And then there's Douglas Adams, author of the best-selling *Hitchhiker's Guide to the Galaxy*. Mr. Adams was the late Mr. Adams long before he died. In fact, such a procrastinator was he that he had to ask his editors to lock him up in New York hotel rooms and hurl threats and insults at him through the door until he slid some pages out to them. Adams made so much money writing that he was able to put it off all he liked. Because of his chronic lateness, he failed to finish his tenth book before his death, leaving it to his editor to finish *The Salmon of Doubt*.

The truth is, procrastination hurts both chronic stallers and those waiting for them to finish. Tim Pychyl, associate professor of psychology at Carleton University, studied students with procrastination problems. He found that they suffered a great deal of anxiety and guilt over projects they had failed to start. Further, Prof. Pychyl (who would have put a real vowel in his name if he'd had time) found that procrastination may even be bad for our health. College students who procrastinate show higher levels of drinking, smoking, insomnia, stomach problems, colds and flu.

With such a steep downside, why does anyone procrastinate?

Let's return for a moment to poor SpongeBob, hunched, paralyzed, over his Boating School paper. If he does a good job, it will move him one step closer to *his most important goal in life*. As numerous episodes make clear, the extroverted SpongeBob longs to have a driver's license. He dreams of driving, gazing with big Bambi eyes at the license in both his hands (leaving none on the steering wheel). Mrs. Puff appears beside him, snatches the license and says, "Not even in your dreams, SpongeBob."

That SpongeBob wants his license so much makes the stakes of this paper high—and then he makes them even higher by instructing himself to make this the best paper ever written. Could this be why SpongeBob is procrastinating? He has set the bar too high, making the Perfect the enemy of the Good. Psychologists studying procrastination have found that perfectionism is often the reason we don't get to work. We feel if it isn't the best paper ever written, or the best quarterly report, or the most outstanding poem, or the cleanest job of toenail painting ever that everyone will think we're stupid and reject us. That's scary. We'd rather not think about it, so we go off and do something else.

Another close ally of procrastination is distraction. Some of us are more easily distracted than others. SpongeBob seizes upon a casual "meow" of his pet snail, Gary, as an excuse to shove back from his essay and feed his pet. When Gary spills a morsel on the floor, SpongeBob sprouts a handle and sponges it up, then notices that the area around the clean spot now looks shabby. He ends up cleaning the whole house, as the clock ticks down on his assignment, until everything gleams like polished chrome. Hint to college boys with papers due: If you are easily distracted, the beach during Sorority Week with all the gorgeous coeds parading past in bikinis is probably not the best place to finish that term paper on the role of salt in early Roman civilization.

Another feature our friends in the white coats have identified in procrastination is our preference for instant (as opposed to delayed) gratification. One famous study showed that poor kids in a ghetto would rather have a Snickers bar now than twenty dollars a week from now. So would Kirstie

Alley, who never lived in a ghetto. In fact, we all tend to pre-fer immediate rewards to pie in the sky. This sheds a lot of light on why we procrastinate. Observe the following graph:

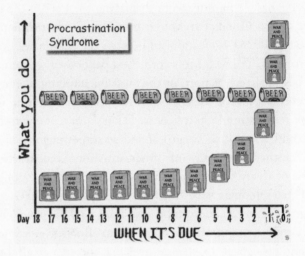

What this graph shows is that, if you've been assigned a paper that's due far off in the future, and you have a choice between working on it tonight or partying, you will be more motivated to party than to start the paper. Partying will go on being the preferred choice until the paper is almost due, and then you will begin to think about your desire to get into medical school so you can use the white coat to get dates, and the way to do that is to finish your paper and get that A. So, on the last night before the paper is due, you are finally more motivated to do it than to party.

What this graph also shows is that you have waited too long and are screwed.

We did not need a graph to show us this, but the author wanted it because it took up half a page and made it look like he had done more work that day.

Let us now get to the bottom line: How to Beat Procrastination.

1. Get it out of your head that you do better under pressure. This is the number-one myth of procrastination. It is false because of the anxiety/performance curve—that inverted "U" we learned about in chapter 4. This curve applies to everyone living. (One of the few advantages of being dead is no anxiety.) If you wait until the last minute, your anxiety level will be so high that the fear will make you stupid and you will do a worse job, not a better one.

2. Don't try to be perfect. Getting a B- or even a C report or task fleshed out is better than doing nothing. You can always fix it up into an A paper after you have a first pass or draft firmly in hand.

3. Divide the project into small parts. This is the most important step in the cure for procrastination. If you don't follow any of the other suggestions, get down with this one. If the professor tells you he wants a report on *War and Peace* in one month, *do not* say to yourself, "Hey, no sweat. It'll take me, what, a couple of days to read *War and Peace*, and a day to do the re-

port." This is wrong. Your heart will tell you it's right, but that is because your heart has no brain and just wants to party and meet hotties. *Do* sit down at once, count the pages in the book and divide by the number of days you have. Save five days at the end to write two pages of report each day.

4. Then—and this is also really important—read each day's little slice first, before you do anything else, preferably even before you get up out of bed and brush your teeth. Why? Because once you have done this you are *free, free, free*! You don't have to think of the book again all day. You don't have to worry if you will get done or get an A. In fact, from the moment you have read today's installment, you are not *permitted* to worry anymore about the project that day. This gives you eleven or twelve waking hours every day of complete freedom from worry about the project, so long as the next morning you again read the day's quota first thing. If you follow this procedure, no task is too large. You can study for comprehensive exams, finish that doctoral dissertation, or write your own novel, *Desire Under the Armpits*, without ever breaking a sweat!

21

KNOWIN' WHEN TO BAIL

And now we get to the yin of timing, procrastination's polar opposite—knowing when to quit. There are more than a few moments in all our lives when we should stop doing what we're doing, cut our losses, throw in the towel, and go on to something else.

SpongeBob is no exception, as we learn when Bikini Bottom decides to have an anchor throw competition. Sponge has very thin arms. Where most people's biceps would be, Sponge is smooth and flimsy as a soda straw. He must struggle to clean and jerk his teddy bear. Sandy Cheeks, his energetic and powerful squirrel friend, puts him on a bodybuilding program; however, Sponge drops out when he realizes he's getting too little gain for all that pain.

Then he sees an ad on TV for inflatable arms. Wow. No

workouts, no high-protein diets, no aching muscles, arms like Bluto. What's not to like? Sponge orders a set of these inflatable arms, straps them on, and goes around Bikini Bottom wowing Larry the Lobster and other muscular competitors for Sandy's admiration. SpongeBob is in heaven. He has solved his problem.

Until Sandy signs him up in the anchor throw.

Right then is the time for him to cut his losses. He should do whatever he has to do to get himself off that list. But we can see no sign he's going to.

In all fairness, knowing when to quit can be a very tricky thing. These days people at the Pentagon are spending billions of dollars and countless sleepless nights trying to hit a bullet with a bullet. On the Pentagon scale of things, this means trying to hit an incoming thermonuclear missile with an outgoing antithermonuclear missile and blow it up before we all must head for that bomb shelter stocked with moldy mattresses and Spam (and hopefully a can opener) that our high school girlfriend's dad dug in his backyard during the height of the Cold War.

The generals and civilians in charge of the missile defense project, after numerous failures to assure a reasonable chance of hitting that missile with a missile, are taking a lot of abuse.

This is not fair.

It is reasonable to ask what chance there is that a North Korean Nero or Iranian Rasputin could really be so crazy as to launch a nuclear-tipped intercontinental ballistic missile at us, when we would simply track it back to its launch point and turn that entire country into a glass parking lot, devoid of all life except cockroaches. It's entirely fair to ask whether spending billions of dollars to prevent such a seemingly unlikely event is the most cost-effective use of taxpayer defense dollars.

What is neither fair nor reasonable is to carp that missile defense can't work because it doesn't yet.

Charles Goodyear had a rubber fetish. The uneducated son of a hardware store owner, Chuck sank over his head in his father's red ink and spent years in debtor's prison. But he was determined to solve the problems that kept rubber from achieving the vital role it now fills in the world's economy and sex lives. Rubber was too sticky. It melted in the summer and froze and cracked in the winter. Goodyear treated rubber with nitric acid and thought he had the problem solved. He sold a lot of rubber stuff in late 1843, but when the long, hot summer of 1844 rolled around, it all melted. This really rubbed his rubber customers the wrong way.

When Chuck got back out of debtor's prison, he tried another process and thought surely he had it this time. So confident was he that he wore rubber suits around town. They got hot and stuck to him. Everyone laughed. Never mind. Goodyear tried again and again. His detractors mocked him. He couldn't even win a rubber of bridge.

And then, beaming back into the past from the starship *Enterprise*, Mr. Spock taught Charles Goodyear how to Vulcanize rubber, and at last Chuck was able to bounce back. No one gave old Charlie a chance. Goodyear had a lot of bad years, and he never reaped a dime from the company founded in his name, but he was right and all his critics were wrong and we're all better off because he didn't cut his losses.

Same with Thomas Edison. On the way to inventing the lightbulb, Tom failed over ten thousand times. To Edison, these were not failures. He liked to say he had discovered more than ten thousand ways not to make a lightbulb. Because of his incredible persistence, we can flip a switch and fill a room with God's own light. Power failures, during which we forget and repeatedly flip that switch, then slap our foreheads in chagrin because no light comes on, are the best moment to appreciate what Edison accomplished because he refused to know when to quit.

None of which explains why SpongeBob is letting the anchor throw draw near without dropping out. He appears to have taken the examples of Goodyear and Edison to heart.

Someone should tell him about Adlai Stevenson.

In 1952, Harry Truman handpicked Adlai to follow him in the job. Adlai went on to win the Democratic nomination and run against fellow bald guy General Dwight Eisenhower. Losing to one of the most popular wartime commanders in U.S. history was no disgrace, but then Adlai did the whole thing over again in 1956, even though he was still Adlai and Ike was still Ike, and Truman was, by then, backing Averell Harriman (no relation to the author). Ike beat Adlai again in part because he still had the best signs, left over from the last time—"I Like Ike." How can you top that? "I'm addled for Adlai" just doesn't have the same ring.

You'd think two losses would be enough for Adlai. And, indeed, in 1960 he didn't openly declare himself a candidate. Instead, Adlai worked hard behind the scenes to persuade the Democratic Convention to draft him as their candidate. He wanted a third try. Turns out he was pitting himself against a fellow Democrat with great hair, a good smile, and an easy first name. John F. Kennedy won his party's nomination and the rest, as they say, is history.

There's a great deal to admire in Adlai Stevenson, but after that first loss to Ike, he might have been happier pursuing a career in acting, like his first cousin McLean. You could do worse than command the 4077th M*A*S*H on a TV show that will pay residuals until the end of time.

If SpongeBob knew how badly refusing to cut his losses worked out for Adlai Stevenson, he might have withdrawn from the anchor toss. Instead he watches with growing dread as the other contestants hurl that anchor down the field. Why doesn't he just walk away, sparing himself the inevitable exposure and humiliation?

Maybe it's unfair to blame a young, inexperienced sponge for making the same mistake as a veteran diplomat and statesman who could have been president if only ten million Republicans had seriously overslept. A more realistic comparison to Adlai might be the wise old salt Eugene Krabs. Mr. Krabs never ran for anything, but he's a man of the world, three-fourths of which, don't forget, is underwater. He owns his own business, and served as head chef on the SS *Diarrhea*. Surely Mr. Krabs knows when to cut his losses.

You can find out if that's really true by reading the following pages.

22

iS THAT YOU?

The night Mr. Krabs must decide whether to cut his losses began that morning, when he woke up feeling old. Looking in his mirror he noticed *multiple* multiple chins. At breakfast, bran, artfully shaped to resemble bacon and eggs, was not enough; daughter Pearl had to throw in a bran pill bigger than Krabs's head.

So when Krabs overhears SpongeBob and Patrick talking at work about the hot night on the town they're planning, he figures it might be just the tonic he needs. He gets himself invited along. That evening, Sponge and Patrick take Krabs to a Laundromat to watch the spin cycle in the dryer, to a maypole around which toddlers are frolicking, and, as an extra added bonus, they all go picking up trash with pointed sticks. Fuming, Mr. Krabs finally decides it's time to cut his losses. He tells Sponge and Pat that they are not cool and that he is going home.

And miss the panty raid? Patrick asks.

Right here is where Krabs should stay with his instincts, turn around, and head for the barn. He's just been through one lame "hot time" after another. He *knows* SpongeBob and Patrick. But a panty raid, awful tempting, hmmmm. . . .

Albert Einstein defined insanity as doing the same thing over and over and expecting a different outcome. Let's take a moment out from Mr. Krabs's little wrestling match with his smarter self to turn our laser-sharp scrutiny on ourselves. What is the number-one thing we humans keep doing over and over, even though we ought to know better? In this never-ending rout of common sense, our losses are measured on the bathroom scale. This is our sacred cow of human irrationality, and our wallets are its cud.

We are, of course, talking about the diet industry.

It rakes in billions of dollars a year persuading us to keep trying to lose weight the industry's way. It has many such "ways," one miracle diet after another, all of which promise we'll get thin and stay thin forever. We are told if we eat no carbs, or if we eat a lot of grapefruit, or if we eat only complex carbs, or if we eat nothing after four p.m., or drink chalky chocolate from cans, or if we replace meals with this supplement or that supplement or buy this line of prepared meals, or that line, or sign up with this group or that group, all of which cost money, we will become svelte gods, and we keep buying and believing and trying. We lose ten or twenty pounds or fifty, then we balloon back up.

Fewer than one in ten of us who lose weight keep it off. Many of the nine regain more than they lost.

How do we break out of this? Do we really want to cut our losses if what we're losing is weight?

If we're among the nine out of ten, the answer is yes. Scientific research into dieting confirms that it's harder on our bodies to lose and regain weight than it is to stay heavy. Few family doctors will tell us this. Maybe it's because they can't be sure we're not that one person out of ten who can make it, instead of the nine out of ten who will be harmed by the advice to diet. Whatever, they keep after us to lose weight, too, because no one can argue that fat is healthy, and our health is our doctors' job, even if they themselves have guts like Ernie Borgnine and stash Slim Jims in their desks with the Viagra and antibiotic samples.

All this Sturm und Drang when we have right in front of us the example of those thin people we so long to resemble. How come no one ever asks them how they do it? Shouldn't they be on TV shows giving their dietary secrets?

The answer is no. Why?

A: Their secret doesn't make anyone any money.

B: Their secret is boring.

C: We actually know what their secret is. They eat less.

Most of them also eat good food, high in nutrition and relatively low in calories. A little meat, a little pasta, a dessert now and then instead of at the end of every meal, a sandwich instead of two sandwiches. They do it day in and day out, nearly every meal, year after year. That's why thin people are thin and why we would be, too, if we decided we wanted to eat like them. The problem with doing this is that it offers no instant weight loss. What's up with that? We want to see the pounds it took us decades to put on melting away in mere weeks. We're in a hurry that never gets us there.

If, instead, we sign ourselves up for a life of regular eating, there will be no ache of starvation at the core of our bones, no little dots swarming before our eyes as we wait for the next hit of calories, no bad breath, no feeling like if we eat another ounce of sausage, or another cheeseburger with no bun or another plate of tofu and rice chips we're going to scream. No boasting how we lost ten pounds in a week, then slinking around feeling ashamed when our banished weight rematerializes on us from its temporary vacation in the fourth dimension.

If we try it the way slim people do it, only two things

FAT CELLS ON VACATION

can happen. We will either stay focused at meals on how much is enough and get thinner very slowly, and thereby change our eating to a sensible pattern over such a long haul that it will engrain itself as our new way of eating . . .

Or we'll fall off eating normally and keep the extra weight.

If so, let us then be at home in ourselves, loved by those who love us, envied by those who envy us, adored by our cats. It's not like Catherine Zeta-Jones or Brad Pitt are going to drop by and jump into bed with us if we lose weight. Being lighter on our feet is a good thing. Eating sensibly (as opposed to dieting) is the best way.

If we find we just can't do that, then let's lose the weight of guilt and misery by getting off our own backs.

Fine, you say, we'll start tomorrow. Now what about Mr. Krabs and the panty raid? Did he cut his losses or did he make a mistake that could lead to years of therapy?

We rejoin Eugene Krabs as he slips into the darkened house with SpongeBob and Patrick. They feel their way along, breathless with anticipation. They find a chest of drawers, and sure enough it is full of panties. Krabs holds them up, laughing with glee. Wow, this is more like it. The two gomers actually came through for him. He was smart not to bail out and go home. . . .

And then Mr. Krabs hears a familiar female voice from his childhood—every child's most familiar female voice: "Eugene, is that you . . . ?"

FAMILY VALUES

THE 6TH WAY

23

No Place Like Home

"There's no place like home."

Judy Garland gave this hoary maxim a fresh coat of quaint in *The Wizard of Oz*, but it doubtless goes back to our earliest ancestors itching to finish the mastodon hunt so they could go home to their significant others, fur beds, and avant-garde cave art. For Dorothy, the epiphany comes as the Wiz beams her back to Kansas, which she never really left. A touching finale and the end of the story because, if the cameras kept rolling, our tears would soon be from boredom. After all, the saying isn't "Home is fun," just that there's no place like it.

In Bikini Bottom, as in Oz, the leading characters have families. With a few noteworthy exceptions, these kinfolk stay offstage. When family issues do enter *SpongeBob*

**DOROTHY IN TOTO
(TOTO ET DOROTHY)**

episodes, they tend to flicker at the edge of vision, then vanish. As when it seems Sponge has actually—hallelujah!—passed his driving test. His parents present his instructor, Mrs. Puff, with a congratulatory cake. Sponge's dad, a genial, rounded fellow, shows a trifle more interest in the Widow Puff than Mom likes. In the next instant, the scene swerves back from this little edge.

We get another fleeting look at Sponge's parents when his pineapple home has been eaten by nematodes and it seems he'll need to move back in with them. The prospect clearly depresses SpongeBob. His folks, for their part, look fatalistic, an expression familiar to the eighty million Americans who've had a grown "kid" show up to reclaim his or her old room before the parents could move to another state and forget to leave a forwarding address.

Then there's SpongeBob's grandma, a sweet lady it seems, until SpongeBob decides he's too old to be kissed and babied by her. The elder sponge accepts this with Zen calm, then turns sadistic, Granny-style, showering Patrick with cookies and knitting him a sweater with love in every stitch to make SpongeBob jealous, then rubbing salt in the wounds by giving Mr. Grown-up SpongeRobert a thick technical manual to read.

Seems wise old Grandma needs Sponge to stay dependent.

By normal family standards, Grandma's plan to make her grandson cry buckets is not really that mean or outrageous. Such crises are the meat and potatoes of home life. Family may mean hugs and kisses and people giving you cake just for aging a year, but it's also where we learn that folks stronger than us will be looking to make us do what they want in life instead of what we want. Family is where we discover we can love someone we don't much like.

That brat of a younger brother, for example, who came along and stole Mom's attention away, even though, as first-born, we were entitled to her undivided love and affection forever. The little scamp was always messing with our things and wanting to tag along, acting all innocent, like he didn't so *ruin* our life. We'd make a game of tying him to a tree, then leaving him there while we took off to play video games. But let anyone else rough him up and we'd be on them like black on eye.

Our parents we had to love, but we passionately disliked Dad that time we were fourteen and he grounded us for a month just for "borrowing" the family station wagon, and, okay, yeah, driving it onto the frozen pond, and doing donuts to impress our buddy. How were we to know the ice would break and the car would sink into three measly feet of water and muck?

Parents, in turn, love their children even as they struggle to stand them—the endless whining, their surly cycles of backtalk and won't-talk, their showing the world at every turn how mortified they are to be seen with us, slipping past with eyes averted, then shrugging off the dread parental grasp when all we wanted was to hug them.

The creators of *SpongeBob* are wise to take care with family issues. Try making family funny and half your audience will be smiling through clenched teeth.

Milking family life for melodrama, on the other hand, is as easy as stomping off to your room, as Will Shakespeare proved over and over in his tragedies. *Antony and Cleopatra* is about a guy trying to get his brother-in-law to be a faithful husband to his sister. In *Coriolanus* the hero wants to sack Rome, but his mom spoils the fun by talking him out of it. Hamlet finds out his uncle killed his dad and married his mom, and it just gets worse from there until everybody who's anybody is dead. Julius Caesar is assassinated in the Forum because he wouldn't listen to his wife and stay home that night. In *King Lear*, the old man disinherits the one daughter out of three who refuses to suck up to him, even though she's also the only one who actually loved him. Macbeth gets into all kinds of trouble because he lets his ambitious wife persuade him to kill his buddy so he can get a better job. Othello ends up croaking his wife for running around on him, and then, after he realizes she was faithful after all, he offs himself, too. *Romeo and Juliet* is about the nasty things that can happen when parents don't approve of their kids' dating choices. Titus Andronicus cuts off his hand in a futile attempt to save his sons, then kills two men who raped his daughter and makes a pie out of them and feeds it to their mother. In *Troilus and Cressida*, Calchus sells out his country to get his ungrateful daughter back from the Greeks. Ten of the eleven Shakespeare tragedies all borrow heavily from family life. Only one didn't, which is why you don't even remember the title: *Timon of Athens*.

And before Shakespeare there was Sophocles, with his *Oedipus the King*, where fate tricks Oed into killing his father and marrying his own mother. Yecch.

You think Shakespeare and Sophocles are too over to have much to say about family? Try *Cat on a Hot Tin Roof* by Tennessee Williams, or the histories of the Hatfields and the McCoys, which show how easily blood ties within families can spill blood between them. In 1890, when historian John Spears (no relation to Britney) visited the abandoned cabin of the patriarch of the Hatfields, he found over the fireplace a lithograph of our opening riff: *There is no place like home*. In the margin, someone who knew about the clan's long and bloody feud had scribbled, "Leastwise, not this side of hell."

24

THiS SiDE OF HELL

In the opening line of *Anna Karenina*, Tolstoy observed: "Happy families are all alike; every unhappy family is unhappy in its own way."

The original draft probably read, "Happy families are boring," but Leo's mama's-boy editor yanked his beard until he changed it. Even in the happiest of families, bad stuff happens. That doesn't mean we'd be better off without them. If you were reasonably lucky, your family took care of your most important needs and gave you the security and love without which you'd have been behind the eight ball all your life. For most of us, even after it's time to go out on our own, our family continues to be the fountainhead of our existence, the source of much good and—best of all—the number-one scapegoat to blame when things go wrong.

We sketched in SpongeBob's family dynamics in the previous chapter. What about the other main characters of the show? Mr. Krabs's home seems happy enough until, over various episodes, we begin to realize it is broken. There's no Mrs. Krabs. Eugene's daughter, Pearl, is a whale, suggesting her mother is too, but no Mrs. Krabs is ever seen and her absence goes unexplained. Maybe, being a mammal, she told Eugene she was going out to get some air and never came back. Krabs talks about his "beloved" mother, and we see her a couple of times, but the crustacean must be largely out of touch with dear old Mum or he'd have recognized her house in the dark that night of the panty raid and saved himself excruciating embarrassment.

In the one episode where the creators of Bikini Bottom did decide to deal head-on with a core pathology of family, they chose not Krabs's family, nor SpongeBob's, but Patrick's. Pat's mom and dad are coming to visit, and this fills him with dread because they don't approve of him. No, it's worse than that—they think he's stupid, and don't mind saying so.

Patrick *can* seem very stupid, as when he trails off and drools in the middle of sentences, or fails to realize that the reason he cannot eat his candy bar is because he already ate it, just a minute ago. In one episode, Patrick takes nearly a minute to learn from SpongeBob how to screw a lid onto a jar. It's unlikely Patrick has any kind of advanced degree, except, possibly, in Human Resources. He has no visible means of support. He lives under a rock, and when he needs an easy chair or a TV set or a lamp, he just sculpts it out of sand. This seems to work fine for him. If he were human rather than a starfish, he'd be a slacker.

Which does not mean he's incapable of insight. When SpongeBob calls him late at night "just to talk," Patrick immediately sees through the charade, telling SpongeBob they both know he is just procrastinating on the paper he's supposed to be writing for Boating School. And that time when he and Sponge decide to adopt the baby clam, Patrick is clever enough to end up with the best role for himself, the "wage earner" who carries a briefcase full of donuts and ice cream and watches TV day and night.

Whatever Patrick's IQ, he is not so stupid that the cutting remarks of his parents don't hurt. Novelist Peter De Vries wrote, "When I can no longer bear to think of the victims of broken homes, I begin to think of the victims of intact ones." Patrick appears to be one of these. That his parents are visiting proves the family still thinks of itself as a unit. But Patrick dreads their presence because he knows they'll make a punching bag out of his fragile self-esteem. That he is almost matter-of-fact when he confides this to SpongeBob somehow makes it all the sadder. It certainly moves SpongeBob, who is so sympathetic he suggests a crazy plan: Sponge will come over while Pat's parents are visiting and act dumb so that Patrick will look smart by comparison.

A lunatic scheme for sure, and yet the problem it is designed to solve is a very real one in both cartoon and human families. Though we might not want to admit it, a lot of us are still trying to please Mom and Dad. They wanted us to be a physician. From their point of view, they've had to lower their sights pretty far to adjust to our actual career of being the guy who sews that little piece of colored yarn into the toes of socks. They handle this disappointment by re-pressing the stark truth and remembering only sewing and feet, and telling everyone back home that we are podiatric surgeons. If we ever go back to the old hometown, we must pray no one stops breathing in the family restaurant our folks frequent, so that public demand won't force us into performing an emergency tracheotomy with our steak knife.

Where does it come from, this great burden of expecta-tion that hangs around our necks and those of our parents? In the next chapter we shall explore these "expect 'taters" in more depth.

25

EXPECT 'TATERS

Jimmy Carter's mother said, "Sometimes when I look at my children I say to myself, 'Lillian, you should have stayed a virgin.'" This was when she was the mother of a sitting president of the United States! Maybe she really only meant her other son, ne'er-do-well Billy, and just lumped Jimmy in with him so Billy wouldn't feel as bad. How nice for Jimmy.

But there's no question that parental "expect 'taters" are spud bombs in the family plot. This subterranean danger is often ignored when experts expound on how families relate to each other, and yet few things could be more important.

Common scenario: By the time Johnny and Mary are two years old, Mom and Dad are pressuring them to get top grades in high school, then go to a good college, and maybe on to grad or law or med school, to land a career that will bring both money and respect to Johnny and Mary, and by extension, glory to the whole clan.

Instead, Johnny gets into women's shoes (and eventually finds work in the field), and Mary marries an insect exterminator, which means her children, if she ever gets around to having any, will probably glow in the dark from all that poison, or have little third hands growing out of the middles of their backs.

And isn't this precisely why we want our kids to do well? Is that so horrid of us?

This is a question only parents ask. The kids who have to deal with the pressure have their answer. But in the abstract, no, it is certainly not wrong to try and motivate your kids toward high-paying careers other than plumbing or being hit men. After all, you are wiser than your kids (at least for the time being), and you just want them to have good and happy lives. You know that while money may not be everything, it can take care of a lot of problems Johnny and Mary may have if they don't get enough of it.

Indeed, quarrels about money and the family budget are a significant cause of unhappiness in marriage. A CBS poll a few years ago found that 84 percent of people making more than $30,000 a year report being happy with their marriage, compared to only 69 percent making less than $30,000. And you also know that if your kids have kids, they'll need even more money. Right now, it costs $7,000 per kid just to get them through their first two years. By the time they're eighteen, this total will have climbed to more than $165,000 per kid, and then there's college—another fifty grand per kid for state public colleges, and more than twice that for private colleges.

So you push Johnny to be a medical doctor and Mary to either be or marry one. Actually, with physicians now paying a hundred grand or more per year just for malpractice insurance, you might better urge your kids to be insurance company executives or tort lawyers.

But here's the thing you might not really have considered, because it would unnerve you too much: What if Johnny and Mary aren't as smart as you think they are?

Wait a minute, you say. We—both their parents—are smart, and they're doing fine in grade school, and Johnny just won the science contest prize for his study of how magnets affect the surface tension of water, so how could they not be smart?

As the words leave your mouth, the alarm bell is ringing at our Fallacy Control Center; our trained statisticians are sliding down their poles dressed in their battle double knits, whipping out their pocket calculators as they sprint for their reeducation trucks.

They are preparing to break it to you that the smarter you and your spouse are, the greater the statistical likelihood that your kids are, to put it bluntly, dumber than you. Patrick's parents know this, and they're only starfish. There are certainly exceptions to this rule in any given family. It's also perfectly true that two people who are smarter than average are likely to have smarter than average kids—just not as smart as them—even as the kids of two parents who have below-average IQs are likely to be smarter than their parents. The principle governing these truths is called "regres-

sion toward the mean" (not "mean" as in "nasty" but as in "average").

But what matters for the question at hand is that, if you and your spouse are real smart, any kids you have are likely to be closer to average IQ than you are. So, just because both of you are MDs or insurance executives or tort lawyers doesn't mean Johnny and Mary can make that grade. And if you're not MDs or insurance executives or lawyers, where do you get off trying to make your kids do it?

26

UNINTENDED CONSEQUENCES

Here's another thing you maybe ought to think about—an unintended consequence of pressuring your kid to achieve. Let's say you and your spouse are both family practice physicians in a small town. Let's say your daughter Mary beats the statistical norm and is smarter than you (though as The Parent, we would never admit that or even believe it could be remotely possible). Say she goes to Harvard, where you had wanted to go but didn't have the grades, and she was graduated summa cum laude when you were happy to make the honor roll at your state college. Mary then goes on to become a brilliant medical researcher at the NIH and discovers a cure for the common cold. Wow, you think. How proud I'd be.

If you're a really good parent and excellent human being, yes.

What about when Mary comes home for a visit, and starts telling you why the way you've been treating patients with canker sores the past twenty years is wrong, and gives you some medical journals so you can read up on it? Is there a gentle and tactful way for her to do that? Or are you, right about then, going to wish Mary had married an insect exterminator and given you the grandchildren, extra hands or no?

Envy and insecurity do not check their knives at the family door. You are probably friends or colleagues with a very nice mother who, it would surprise you to know, can draw an ounce of blood with an envelope. She does it by addressing her daughter's birthday card to "Mrs. George Miller." Her daughter has a Ph.D. in biology and is a full professor. If a title is used with her name alone, the correct title is "Dr." But each year, on the date this lovely and well-mannered mother brought her daughter into the world, she denies her daughter's highest accomplishment—and every scrap of her personal identity—before the daughter can even get to the pretty sentiments inside the card.

You may also know a fine, upstanding father who, it would surprise you to learn, never asks his son about his job, even though Dad worked all his life as a loan officer in the bank of which the son is now a vice president. The father will, as he always has, volunteer advice to his son on every subject, but he will bring up nothing that might draw notice to the fact that, were he still at the bank, his son would be his boss. The crime of the biologist daughter and the banker son is that they got too big for their britches.

This might actually be Patrick Star's crime too, literally if not figuratively. When his parents visit, we see no sign that they have done better than, or even as well as, their son. But the condescension and the snide little digs arrive with them at the door. SpongeBob appears on cue. Acting clumsy and inarticulate, he stumbles around blurting out odd noises and running into things. Patrick's parents find this hilarious—and pitiable. The heat is off Patrick and onto his scapegoat. The plan seems to be working!

And then it jumps the tracks. As Patrick joins Mom and Dad in laughing at poor, dumb SpongeBob, he begins to feel at long last like he's really one of the family. Here they are all doing something together, all of them on the same side for once. Patrick starts heaping the put-downs on SpongeBob with way too much zeal, and Sponge starts to resent it. Peeved, he drops his stupid act, but it's too late. At this point, nothing he could do will convince Mom and Dad Star that he's anything but an idiot.

Has Sponge's sacrifice really changed anything?

Never fear, the episode has a big twist yet to come. To give it away here would spoil the fun for those who have not seen it. Let's just say that, by the end, the family "expect 'taters" have been unearthed and exposed as a bad deal for all concerned.

Unfortunately, in human families, there are few resolutions as neat as Patrick's. The rift between mother and biologist daughter, father and banker son, can't very well heal when no one will talk about it. The daughter would feel she's being petty if she must ask her mother for the respect anyone else would give her. The son can't say to his dad, "Don't you even want to know what I'm doing at the bank?," because if you have to ask, you have your answer already.

The Bible doesn't tell us how Joseph felt when Jesus blew off the family carpentry business to go take a shot at becoming the Messiah. We can imagine a hurt Joseph saying to himself, "What's carpentry, chopped liver?" Resentment and envy of our grown offspring can happen only when we, as parents, didn't understand what we were supposed to be doing when they were little. Our job was neither to make them into doctors or lawyers, nor to withhold that encouragement if it's where they want to go. However much we might like to forever keep them as our children, our duty is to *raise* them, which means lift them up so they can go out as adults and be happy and effective in the world. On the day we ourselves came into the world, we knew nothing and our parents were our gods. In the next two decades, it was our job to outgrow our gods and take over our own lives. Now, as parents, it's our duty to step our authority back from our kids at the right moments and finally stand down when our job is done. This is one of the toughest passages in all of life—for the parents to willingly give up status and power, and for the kids to muscle up to the job of outgrowing the gods of infancy.

If you're sixteen, seventeen, or eighteen right now, and home life is so good and comforting you're not sure you want to leave and go out on your own, here's a little parable for you. It's about the dog, the fence, and the snowstorm. The fence is three and a half feet high. It keeps the family dog in the backyard so it can't run around and rough up the neighbor's cat or turn over garbage cans. The fence has served this purpose for years, and the dog has gotten used to it. He peers through the wire every day and thinks about how neat the world out there looks. But he knows he can't get over the fence, and the backyard is, after all, pretty nice. Then it snows, and keeps on snowing until there's two feet of the stuff, packed down. And there the dog is, still sitting inside the fence. Because the fence has always been impassable, the dog does not question it now, even with the evidence before its eyes. It does not recognize that it can now step over the fence and explore the world beyond its backyard—and that it can also step back when it wants to, and get the good things of home and its own backyard.

If that's the kind of kid you are, get ready. It will soon be time to step over, Rover.

If we understand the family's primary reason for being, we find that its most central problems begin to make sense. Maybe the mother doesn't want to write "Dr. Glenda Miller" on her daughter's birthday card because it makes her feel like her own bachelor's degree, quite a feat in its time, is inadequate. Or because raising Glenda was the best and noblest thing she ever did, and she doesn't want it to be over, and writing "Dr." on the card has taken on that meaning for her. The cure, if you're the mom, is to realize that the "Dr." in front of your daughter's name is your achievement too, a grand tribute to your motherhood. And if you're the daughter, you cut Mom some slack, because you understand that the address on the card isn't really because she doesn't respect you, but because she's afraid if she respects you too much, you won't respect her anymore.

Fortunately, in a blessed few families, the intricate dance of power and expectation between parents and their offspring will proceed in a manner so graceful, so filled with mutual respect, that you will have the great good fortune of being boring to the rest of us. Your reward is that the Leo Tolstoys of today will bypass you and expose all the dirty little secrets of some other family to the world.

And if your family is not 100 percent perfect, maybe you're using the wrong yardstick. Clarence Darrow said, "The first half of our lives is ruined by our parents and the last half by our children." By that measure, most of us are doing pretty well, even Patrick, who after all is making it just fine. His parents, whoever they are, must have done something right.

THE 7TH
WAY

THEOLOGY

27

PRIDE GOETH BEFORE A FALL

The Seventh Way to happiness, SpongeBob-style, is through theology.

Which we will define here as "what you believe about God."

With one rather remarkable exception, which we'll save for last, *SpongeBob* episodes are not implicitly about theology. At the same time, many do illustrate theological principles. As does all humor, theological humor involves slipping on the banana peel instead of stepping around it, so we learn from SpongeBob and friends what not to do as much as what to do.

In SpongeBob's world, a little humility is a boon to happiness, just as most religions teach. Proverbs 16:18 in the Christian Old Testament says, "Pride goeth before a fall, and a haughty spirit before destruction." Here, "fall" is probably meant symbolically, as in: you were so sure you landed the Blimsberg account that you went around telling everyone in the Farkle Ad Agency it was in the bag, and then Blimsberg went to your competitor Finster, and your boss, who had earlier bought you high-priced champagne and told everyone how smart you were, fired you. Whether he would have fired you had you not strutted around like the NBC Peacock raising everyone's expectations isn't clear, but the show of hubris definitely made being fired feel even worse. And there's no doubt pride went before your metaphoric fall.

In a TV episode of *The West Wing*, people in the White House Communications Office are getting ready to have a party celebrating the Senate's confirmation of the president's nominee for the Supreme Court. As the vote is going on, Toby Ziegler, dour head of communications, comes in and catches his staff pouring champagne. He gets very mad and takes all their glasses and bottles away and lectures them about not celebrating until it's a done deal. When he is finished haranguing them, they all look as glum as he does all the time, and he is happy.

Basically, Ziegler is warning his staff about hubris—pride that offends the gods. The hubris of others almost always precedes a fall of some kind, if only in our wishful thinking. SpongeBob proves no exception in an episode about shoe tying. This episode demonstrates that pride can come before a literal fall. Patrick brings his new shoes to show SpongeBob. Sponge asks him to try them on, and Patrick confesses that he doesn't know how to tie his shoes.

Patrick is not afflicted with the sin of pride. He can admit when he doesn't know something.

Alas, SpongeBob is smitten with pride that he, indeed, can tie his shoes and will now show Patrick how it's done. He does not simply say, "Here, buddy, watch this and you'll be doing it in no time." Oh, no, he has to gloat about his prowess, strut a little and assure Patrick that he is about to learn from the master.

And then, of course, he blows it.

Turns out SpongeBob has been wearing those shoes since he was a sperm. Sperm have no arms or hands, which means he never tied them in the first place. After confidently untying both shoes, he realizes he has no idea how to tie them again. Patrick, with some understandable relish, suggests that maybe SpongeBob doesn't know how either. This is Sponge's chance to humble himself, to say, "I seem to have forgotten," but no. The fact that he acted so superior has now trapped him, and he can't admit that he is not a master knotsman after all. Fortunately for SpongeBob, Patrick remembers he has to be somewhere else and Sponge's shame remains secret—for the moment. Sleeping on it doesn't help. When he tries to go to work the next morning, he falls fifteen times, tripping on his laces, each pratfall recorded on camera. Because of his pride.

Deborah Tannen, a professor of linguistics at Georgetown University, when interviewed about her book *You Just Don't Understand*, said that one of the biggest complaints she gets when she researches people's frustration with their bosses is managers who won't admit when they don't know something or aren't sure of it. As a result, employees waste a lot of time on work they wouldn't have pursued if the boss had admitted up front he wasn't sure it could pan out. Pride and not wanting to appear weak are both factors in not admitting when you're wrong. In fact, Tannen says, more often than not, admitting you're wrong and apologizing leaves a very powerful positive impression.

One of the nastier falls in ancient history that followed too much pride was what happened to Hezekiah, king of Israel, back around 700 B.C. Hez had been sick, and Berodachbaladan, the son of Baladan, king of Babylon, wrote him a letter asking how he was doing. For being so sweet, Hezekiah invited him for a visit. Berod (let's call him that for short) was a pretty sly character. Apparently, he flattered Hezekiah, kept oohing and aahing, egging Hez on as the Israelite king took him around and showed off all his wealth, silver and gold, his armor, everything he had. Look at me, am I not grand?

With that special snooping radar no prophet should be without, Isaiah then dropped in on Hezekiah. Isaiah was probably toting a pretty big bale of his own pride, being that he spoke for God. (This same malady now afflicts Senate staffers.) Being God's mouthpiece, Isaiah never minced words with Hezekiah just because he was a king. He asked Hezekiah what he'd shown Berod, and Hezekiah proudly answered, "Pretty much everything."

"You idiot," Isaiah said. "Now he's gonna come back and take it all away from you and carry it and your people off to Babylon, and on top of that, he's gonna whip out his short knife and make all your sons into eunuchs."

Ouch.

What Isaiah predicted happened. Never before or since has pride cost a man so much, or at any rate, his sons.

The moral of that very old story is, of course, that if Hezekiah had said, "Hey, Berodachbalawhatchamacallit, instead of you coming to the palace, why don't I just meet you at the Fig Tree restaurant in Jerusalem and I'll buy you a nice lunch, or better yet, I'll come to Babylon and you can show me all your stuff, which I'm sure must be truly awesome?"

Maybe Berod wouldn't have bought it, but at least Hezekiah's sons could have kept the family jewels, not to mention Jerusalem not having to get sacked by the Babylonians.

If there's a lesson for today, it's that people probably like you more if you don't flaunt all your toys and goodies, and if you admit when you're wrong. It'll throw people. The ones with brains will think you're stronger, not weaker.

Your sons are probably safe either way.

28

LiFE SENTENCES

A tenet of all major religions is to love your neighbor. Sounds nice, but the principle definitely goes against our tribal and clannish roots. Our predecessor, Cro-Magnon man, was so kind to neighboring Neanderthals that Cro and his head-knocking lads wiped out that other human race.

Nowadays, of course, we're much better about loving our neighbor. We do our best to make sure people who aren't like us don't get into the neighborhood. The people who do get in have our affection, or at least our tacit acceptance, so long as they shovel their front walks when it snows, keep up their lawns, and don't paint their house the wrong color.

Not exactly what Jesus meant by "Love thy neighbor as thyself."

A tall order, to be sure.

An episode of *SpongeBob* shows us what might come from truly loving our neighbor. Being that the neighbor in question is Squidward, much of the episode isn't pretty. When Mr. Krabs can't find the first dime he ever made, he accuses Squidward, who keeps the Krusty Krab cash register, of stealing it. Squidward, deeply offended, quits his job, confident he can find work more suited to his talents.

When next we see him, he's living in a cardboard box on the street, begging from passersby and sporting a very unbecoming beard. Sponge, appalled that his old friend and neighbor should have become this broken-down, whining husk with zero confidence, takes Squidward in, gives him his bed, brings him meals, and even polishes his bald dome to a high sheen.

Sponge's reward for this, as the days pass, is that Squidward, after some initial thanks, becomes a tyrant, ringing the bell constantly for this or that task he wants his host to perform. It may seem SpongeBob is a sap for putting up with Squidward's outrageous behavior. He seems to get nothing back for his kindness—unless we rise above the immediate situation and consider how we feel about Sponge-Bob for being the way he is, not just in this episode but over all of them.

We love him. He is kind, slow to anger, energetic, determined to be a friend to anyone who will let him (even Plankton), funny, and unfailingly upbeat. SpongeBob's reward for the way he treats Squidward is the kind of sponge it makes of him, and the way everyone responds to him because of that.

Heck, they even gave him his own show.

So what do you do when you go to bed at night, pull the covers up to your chin, close your eyes, and the neighbor's dog starts barking?

You're lying there, feeling your eardrums pulse with each bark—it seems the dog was a teenager in its former life, cut down just as his voice was changing, and reincarnated as a canine that can simultaneously bark in two different registers, the upper of which sounds like tires screeching on pavement. You lie in bed, feeling your pulse speed up, your teeth clench.

You may not realize it, but at this moment you are also talking to yourself. Maybe you are saying something like this: "That bastard Peterman, doesn't he hear that dog? He's got to hear it, but he just doesn't care. He's letting the dog bark because he's still up, so he doesn't give a damn whether anyone else can get to sleep. Inconsiderate bastard, I'm gonna call the cops on him."

Now two things are happening. The dog is barking and you are making yourself even madder by what you are telling yourself.

The good news is that famed shrink Albert Ellis pioneered a school of therapy just for you. Step one is to figure out what sentences you are saying to yourself that are, in turn, whipping your emotional system into an exaggerated frenzy.

Note the difference between these two sentences:

1. That Peterman doesn't give a damn about his neighbors.

2. Maybe Peterman can't hear the dog because he's got his earphones on.

Sentence one sends your blood pressure skyrocketing, and sentence two suggests that there might be a solution to your problem that does not involve high-powered rifles, all the blood rushing to your face, and the torching off of a war that will make the Hatfields and the McCoys look like Tim the Toolman and Wilson.

If you're telling yourself sentence one, you'll probably end up mounting a big klieg light on the back of your house and pointing it straight at Peterman's bedroom window, prompting him to go out and buy a high-powered rifle himself. If you're telling yourself sentence two, you might just decide to write Peterman a note that goes something like this. "Dear Joe, you're a terrific neighbor, and that's a great dog you've got there. I imagine you're a sound sleeper, which is good. Unfortunately, I'm hearing Spot when he

161

goes out at night and barks. I'm wondering if you'd be so kind as to shut the dog door when you go to bed at night, just between, say, ten at night and five in the morning. That would be so great. Here's a cake Phyllis baked for you. Hope you enjoy. Warmly, Milo."

Then if Joe doesn't keep the dog quiet at night, shoot the son of a bitch.

No, seriously, if the nice note doesn't work, there are other things you can do, like get that machine that makes noise like rain or the ocean, or replace your single-pane windows with double- or triple-paned ones to seriously cut down how much noise gets through. And most important of all, you don't tell yourself things that make your feelings about the situation worse.

Your reward will be the same as SpongeBob's. People will like you more and bake cakes for you and elect you president of the neighborhood association and all the women on the block will think you're wonderful, and even if none of that happens, you'll be calmer, more in control, and you will like yourself as much as you like SpongeBob.

29

BELIEVING IS BELIEVING

If happiness through theology were simple and self-explanatory, there'd be no need for further tips in any book, but as we have seen in the sad case of people who believe they are charitable but give nothing to charity, believing is not the same as doing. For most of us, believing is believing.

As noted earlier, one episode of *SpongeBob* is slyly theological in its tone. While it never mentions religion as such, most viewers familiar with religion would find the references hard to miss. Basing an episode on religion is pretty daring of the creators of *SpongeBob*, given that old adage about the perils of discussing theology or politics. We humans tend to be at our touchiest on these two subjects. We can imagine that when the creators of *SpongeBob* met to discuss whether they should do an episode on theology, the following conversation took place:

"Hey, uhm, why don't we do an episode on religion?"

"Is that a rhetorical question?"

"What's a rhetorical question?"

"It's like when I ask 'Why are you so stupid?' and I'm not asking because I expect to be answered but because it's my way of calling you stupid, and then you try to answer anyway."

"Oh." Long pause. "Because when I was little, Mommy dropped me on my head."

Whether or not this was the verbatim conversation, as soon as the decision was made, the entire staff of cartoonists, storyboarders, writers, voice actors and directors took out life insurance policies and put false addresses and phone numbers in any database with personal information about them.

The "theology" episode of *SpongeBob* begins innocently enough: Sponge and Patrick are playing in their tree house when who but Squidward should happen by on his bike. He asks what they are doing, and they tell him it's a secret club and they're sorry but there isn't any room for him to join. This, of course, is like pouring lighter fluid on simmering coals, which you are not supposed to do unless you're into the totally hairless look.

In a series of events worthy of a Rube Goldberg machine, Squid shimmies up the tree and ends up catapulting himself, Sponge, and Pat far out into a dark, sinister kelp jungle.

So far this episode might or might not be about theology. True, the club has its own special language and is strict about what it requires of members. But we're not sure the unfolding story is really about religion until the three are marooned and SpongeBob whips out his Magic Conch Shell.

Sponge explains that the "brothers" in the club consult the Conch before making any decision. (It has a string you pull, like the ones in talking dolls. As the string retracts, the Conch speaks.) Sponge asks the Conch what they should do and it says, "Nothing." So Patrick and SpongeBob sit down in the little clearing and go still with a trancelike calm. Disgusted, Squid tries to find his own way home without them. He soon becomes lost, panics, and ends up back in the little clearing where he left Sponge and Pat. There they still sit, where he left them, the same serene looks on their faces.

Is this a statement on the silliness of faith or the smartness of it?

Squidward thinks trusting a "magic" conch is moronic. Squid would rather run around, flapping his arms and legs and panicking, staying lost despite all his efforts. Sponge and Patrick are just as lost as Squidward, but they don't feel lost. They are not afraid. They feel secure and serene because, in this strange big world, this wilderness, they have faith.

At this point, the atheists among us are probably asking, "What if I can't believe? Christians, Jews, Muslims, and all other believers in a deity would agree their God is who gave man his brain. What if, using that brain, you have thought and thought about whether God exists and just found it too far-fetched?" Is our faithless atheist supposed to say he believes when he does not, and thereby become a hypocrite? And if he were to say he believes, while he really doesn't because he just can't, how can such a fake faith work for him?

(These questions are, of course, rhetorical. But if you wish to reply, run off a hundred copies of your answer and mail or fax each one separately to the people who keep mailing and faxing us invitations to that "free" vacation down in Florida.)

Back in the kelp forest, Squid taunts the two true believers, calling them idiots for putting their faith in the Magic Conch, just sitting there, waiting for food to magically appear from the sky.

And then food does magically appear from the sky, as a plane full of picnic supplies must jettison its load. Praising the Magic Conch, Sponge and Pat chow down, while Squidward, starved after days in the jungle, stares with longing at the food. He asks, would it be all right for him to eat, too?

Let's ask the Conch, SpongeBob suggests.

Squidward keeps yanking the Conch's string but It refuses at every pull to let him eat. So, therefore, do Sponge and Patrick.

We now have enough from this episode to examine which banana peels SpongeBob, Squidward, and Patrick slipped on, and how spotting those slippery devils and stepping around them would have led to greater happiness for all concerned.

First off, Squidward the atheist was way out of line for mocking Sponge and Patrick's religion. There's a word for this, and it's "rude." In reality, most atheists are decent enough folk. Secular humanism, which is what many atheists believe in, has a lot of admirable qualities. It emphasizes individual freedom and responsibility, human values of love and compassion, and the need for tolerance and cooperation for the good of all. Nowhere in these beliefs is anyone encouraged to act superior, mock religion, call those who practice it stupid, or just generally get in people's faces with a lot of hoity-toity intellectual reasons why there is no God. Once, just once, we'd like to see them get struck by lightning while they're saying that, but as the scriptures say, the Lord causes the rain to fall on the wicked and the righteous alike.

Squidward was rude, but the true believers in this story aren't blameless either.

Researchers at the University of Houston did a survey a short time ago. One of the questions was: "Should a community allow its civic auditorium to be used by atheists who

want to preach against God and religion?" Of the respondents, 17 percent said yes, 13 percent said it depends (gotta give the wishy-washy a place to go), and 70 percent said no. When the question was, "Should a community allow its civic auditorium to be used by Protestant groups who want to hold a revival meeting?," the numbers flip-flopped, and 68 percent said yes. In case you think the people who took this survey weren't fair-*minded*, 89 percent of them agreed with the following statement: "I believe in free speech for all no matter what their views might be."

Just not in my civic auditorium.

Sadly, this survey is more evidence that how people see themselves ("I believe") doesn't match up very well with what they would actually do ("should a community allow"). When SpongeBob's and Patrick's faith was justified and the food came tumbling, mannalike, from the heavens, they flunked the next test of their own beliefs. Most religions, like atheism, teach tolerance and cooperation, and even go one better in advocating that we be good to those who are nasty to us. The Bible, the Koran, and many other sacred texts teach that, if your enemies are hungry, feed them. If they are thirsty, give them something to drink.

Let's assume the reason the Magic Conch (which it's pretty clear represents prayer) wouldn't give Squidward any food is that he was just jerking the string; that he didn't know how to pray and, in any case, didn't have the belief to make it work for him. Does that mean SpongeBob and Patrick should deny him the food, as they did? No. If their religion is superior, it forgives Squidward and feeds him.

Be we atheist, Christian, Buddhist, Muslim or of any

other mind, we will be happier if we act on what we believe instead of just believing it. No true religion teaches that we should be at each other's throats. It's just as wrong to insist that everyone go around saying "Merry Christmas" instead of "Happy Holidays" as it is to mock God and religion.

The Seventh Way to happiness is that we can all get through life together if we stay out of each other's faces, practice a little humility, try to love our neighbors, and help each other when possible.

In short, we live up to what we say we believe.

THE 8TH WAY

GETTING ALONG WITH OTHERS

30

THE MAN(TA) iN THE STREET

SpongeBob's Eighth Way to happiness is about getting along with others, as Sponge does so well. Working our way in from Pluto (total stranger) to the Sun (you), "others" includes casual acquaintances, neighbors, coworkers and people we socialize with on the Internet, and, finally, friends. How to get along with your family would take another whole book. In contrast, the secret to a good relationship with your significant other is simpler than getting batteries out of those thick, hermetically sealed plastic packages. Just make sure you always treat your sweetheart like your best friend.

Let's start with the strangers you pass on the street. In Bikini Bottom it would be fish with legs. As many episodes make clear, SpongeBob is at one with strangers. He has a good time trying to sell chocolate door to door, though he buys more stuff from his "customers" than he sells. He's onstage every chance he gets, singing, playing the guitar, doing stand-up, and stylin' with his mop. Though sponges can't swim, he bluffs his way into lifeguard duty so beach crowds will admire him—with scary results (though one wouldn't think a starfish could drown). Sponge competes in the annual fry cook games, and when Mr. Krabs's daughter, Pearl, is stood up by her prom date, Sponge gladly stands in, though all her school friends are strangers to him. (Wearing a tux and stilts to measure up to the debutante whale, he becomes the center of attention, and let us just say he has to take Pearl home early.) Sponge appoints himself a sort of Paul Revere for Santa Claus, stirring up the whole town over Santa's very iffy coming. SpongeBob fakes a fight in an effort to show the bouncer he's tough enough to get into a saloon full of we-bad strangers. Saying hello to everyone he passes in the street is what plunges SpongeBob into an existential crisis we'll examine in this book's final chapters.

Not everyone can be as stranger-friendly as Sponge-Bob. But a certain modest effort feels good to most of us and helps keep society's gears greased. The book on getting along with strangers is pretty simple, so long as you haven't crash-landed in certain remote jungles of New Guinea, or don't move from New York City to, say, Muscatine, Iowa.

Since the latter is more likely than the former, a word on moving from New York to Muscatine: Introverts make up about 30 percent of the human population. You'd think they'd avoid the world's capital of overstimulation, New York City, but they don't. Like most people, introverts need jobs and there are lots of jobs in the Big Apple. Also, introverts who have not read this book may not realize they are introverts and that they therefore need to be in a calm, quiet place with lots of space around them.

Surprisingly, it was the introverts of New York City who long ago established the minimalist street manners of all New Yorkers. They brought off this remarkable feat without meaning to, over time, through a psychological process called "shaping." Back when the first pedestrian crawled from the primordial ooze of First Avenue, the fledgling extroverts of the city would look everyone in the eye as they passed and say "how aw ya?" Seventy percent of the time, the other person would be an extrovert and would say "how aw ya?" back. However, the three out of ten introverts would look startled, refuse to make eye contact, and hurry past. This was very punishing to the extroverts, who like the stimulation of mixing it up with other people even if they don't care a fig about them.

A curious fact of psychology is that if you get randomly punished part of the time for doing something, you'll find that more disturbing than if you get punished every time. This is because, whether something is good or bad, we like it to be predictable. Inconsistency makes us nauseous. If you know you're going to get an electric shock every time you open a door, at least you don't have to worry, on top of the pain, whether this will be the time.

Of course, the smart thing might be to stop going through that door, but we can't, because 95 percent of our DNA is identical to a monkey's and we need to see what's on the other side.

So anyway, the extroverts of New York City started worrying whether this person they wanted to greet was going to be the one that punished them by withholding stimulation. To avoid that little shock, they stopped greeting anyone. This did not mean the introverts won. The extroverts get even by standing too close to the introverts on elevators.

Now, if a New Yorker were to move to Muscatine and not say hello when a town citizen passed him on the sidewalk, he might well find the greeting repeated until he must either return it or risk being mired in an ugly scene. People in Muscatine are more friendly because they have a lot more personal space and less crime, and because they burned all their introverts in wicker cages years ago for not saying hello.

There's such a thing as being too much in the face too, as SpongeBob illustrated when he went around ripping his pants in front of strangers for laughs. It worked for a while, but he ran it into the ground. Better to hang back a little.

You can smile at people, but don't stare, especially at gorgeous women who are with guys wearing leather jackets, tattoos, and shoulder holsters. It's good to open doors for other people regardless of sex and age. Just make sure first that they want to go through the door. In cars, you may not make any gestures at another person, stare at him, follow him at high speeds within a foot of his bumper or cut him off in traffic. The reason is not that he might have a .357 magnum under the seat (though that is an excellent reason). The reason is that it isn't good for you, him, or the rest of us who are just trying to get wherever we're going. Your blood pressure goes up, you accomplish nothing positive, you will suffer heart palpitations and an embarrassing tremor in your hands for an hour afterward, and even if you don't get shot, every single time you will later wish you didn't do it.

What else?

Oh—you know to turn your cell phone off in theaters and concerts and church, right? And in restaurants you don't talk any louder on your phone than you would to a person sitting at your table. See, the phone has little speakers and microphones and such that magnify your voice, and if the party you're calling is a hundred miles away, it won't help to shout in any case.

31

THE 'HOOD

Next we'll discuss getting along with neighbors and other acquaintances, including those from the Internet.

One episode of *SpongeBob SquarePants* is remarkable for starring pretty much the whole neighborhood of Bikini Bottom. As we'd expect, Mrs. Puff is there, Plankton, Larry the Lobster, Patrick, SpongeBob, Mr. Krabs, and his daughter, Pearl, but also many of the town's wallflowers, who heretofore have stayed in the background as street extras and dining patrons at the Krusty Krab.

What has brought them all together?

A neighborhood organizer named Squidward.

What, you ask, could have turned introvert Squidward into a neighborhood organizer? The answer is his high school classmate and supercilious fellow squid Squilliam.

Squilliam presents himself as everything Squidward dreams of being but has failed to become—rich, musically success-ful, handsome, well-dressed, adored. To taunt Squidward, Squilliam calls and confides that his top-rated band was asked to play in the prestigious Bubble Bowl, but he has to be elsewhere that day. Could Squidward fill in with his own band? Squidward does have a band, doesn't he, like he bragged he would have back in high school?

Or is he maybe laboring, bandless, in the trenches of the food services sector?

Terrified of admitting to Squilliam that he does, indeed, operate a cash register in a hash house, Squidward agrees to bring "his band" and fill in. He has no band, so he plasters handbills all over the neighborhood, promising fame, free food, and other goodies if his neighbors and fellow towns-people will come to the rehearsal hall on the appointed night. He rents instruments, hands them out when the neighbors arrive, and undertakes to mold them into a band, despite the fact that none of them admits to having played an instrument before.

How interesting that he who blows off his neighbors suddenly needs them to blow on his rental horns. And how intriguing that they respond. We'd understand them rally-ing to help SpongeBob, who has involved himself in their lives in a friendly way at every turn. But they come out for Squidward, too—even the shy introverts of Bikini Bottom. Clearly, socializing is not just for the bold.

Since the first caveman Og hit his neighbor Ig with a stick for coming around too often to trade grunts, people have varied in how—and how much—they socialize. Og might have hit Ig because Og was an early introvert and Ig a prototype extrovert who was too much in his face, but that doesn't mean Og was entirely unsociable. Maybe Og wanted to socialize but couldn't because the Internet hadn't been invented yet.

The invention of the Internet is cool partly because it opened up a new social arena, one of the few that is tailor-made for introverts. The Net gets knocked for isolating people from each other, but as actual users know, this is bunk. Oh, sure, there are a few sad addicts who cruise the Net day and night, never going anywhere "real," until someone gets worried, and their landlady lets the police in and only the addict's feet remain, sticking out of the monitor. But most of us cruise in addition to our normal lives.

Sarah Birnie and Peter Horvath of Acadia University in Canada studied 115 undergrad men and women and found that "shyness was associated with increased intimate social-

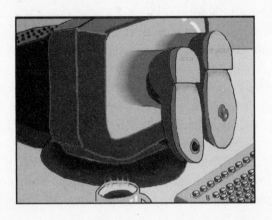

izing over the Internet." Their study also demonstrated that extroverts are hardly closed out—they, too, use the Internet to socialize, and it doesn't turn them into hermits. In fact, Internet socializing often leads to actual face-to-face meetings that would not otherwise have occurred. Dr. Jeff Gavin (University of Bath) studied couples who met for the first time online and went on to spend time establishing a relationship through e-mailing each other and talking in chat rooms. When these couples then screwed up their nerve to actually meet, 94 percent of them went on to see each other again. Most people reading this book know a couple that got married after meeting on the Internet.

This chapter isn't long enough for an extended discussion of getting along with others on the Internet. One tip will have to suffice: If you look more like Ernest (goes to camp) than Brad (Achilles) Pitt, and you plan to meet the woman you're talking to online, don't post photos of Brad Pitt and say you look like him only handsomer.

There's no sign the Internet has reached Bikini Bottom. Maybe that's why even the town introverts responded to the chance for a little socializing when one of their own stepped up to organize it. At the start, Squidward is sure he has enough talent for all of these self-confessed nonmusicians. The fledgling band immediately sets out to prove him wrong. The percussion section tries to play drums by blowing on the sticks. Tiny Plankton, assigned to the harmonica, soon runs out of breath dashing up and down to blow in its holes. The band gets into arguments and fights when it should be practicing. When a brawl consumes the much-needed final practice session, Squidward gives up in despair, tells the band they've destroyed him, and prepares to endure Squilliam's scorn.

And that is when Squidward's next-door neighbor, SpongeBob, steps up. Sponge asks the band to imagine that Squidward would carry them from their burning home, or resuscitate them if they took too many tanning pills and stopped breathing.

He asks them to imagine that Squidward is a good neighbor.

Experts on road rage tell us that a large part of what permits us to lose our tempers and act like maniacs toward other drivers is that we can't see them. They are hidden away in the capsule of the car, anonymous, dehumanized. A recommended therapy is to imagine that the person in a car that has started to annoy you is someone you know and like. You visualize a neighbor or friend who would never deliberately annoy you. In other words, you make a faceless irritant into a real person, a nice individual like yourself.

In capturing the imaginations of Squidward's neighbors and filling them with good images of a poor, desperate soul, SpongeBob is doing nothing less than applying the glue that sticks us all together into one big halfway happy society. If you're having trouble getting along with a neighbor, you might try visualizing him as a friend of a friend, a person who is worth at least a hello, or a helping hand as you pass by. That's all Sponge asked of the band—not to become Squidward's close personal friends but to see him as worth helping. When the good folk of Bikini Bottom did that, their reward was that it made their lives better, too.

32

FRiENDS AND FiENDS

George Canning, prime minister of England in the early 1800s, and veteran of lots of sharp-elbowed fights in Parliament, wrote the following little ditty about friendship, in which we should forgive his clumsy attempts to sustain meter on the grounds that it is hard to be both a prime minister and a decent poet:

> *Give me the avowed, the erect, the manly foe,*
> *Bold I can meet,—perhaps may turn his blow!*
> *But of all plagues, good Heaven, thy wrath can send,*
> *Save, save, oh save me from the candid friend!*

Awkward meter or no, the sentiment rocks. We all have an overly candid friend. The one who gives us antiperspirant for our birthday or tells us we'd be beautiful if we'd just lose that forty pounds. We know we hate this. What we may not be so quick to realize is whether we are ever like this.

Of course we aren't. When we advise our friend Max that he's too butt-ugly to date a stunner like Trixie, we are only trying to spare his feelings down the line when Trixie would be sure to come to that inevitable conclusion herself. And when Max showed us the cartoon he planned to send to the *New Yorker* and we stared at it without smiling and said, "Is that supposed to be a man or a woman?," we were only offering constructive criticism in an effort to help him realize his dream of someday being as funny as we are.

The number-one candid friend in Bikini Bottom has to be Patrick. As we'll see in the penultimate chapter of this book, he doesn't hesitate to suggest SpongeBob is ugly. He immediately slaps down Sponge's attempt to distract himself from his homework with a little friendly conversation. When SpongeBob's pet snail, Gary, shows a preference for Patrick, Mr. Sensitivity calls Sponge's attempts to win back his pet's affection "pathetic," and solemnly informs Sponge that he had every chance to be the one Gary prefers and he failed. In another episode, SpongeBob persuades Patrick to come watch a giant clam do tricks. When the sleeping clam just lies there, Patrick says, "Boring. Thanks for nothing."

So what's wrong with that? Isn't being totally honest what friends do?

Thankfully, the research says otherwise. W. Keith Campbell of Case Western Reserve University, Constantine Sedikides of the University of Southampton, Glenn D. Reeder of Illinois State University, and Andrew J. Elliot of the University of Rochester somehow stumbled upon each other and did a cool study. Writing it up in the *British Journal of Social Psychology* (2000 [39, pp. 229–39]), they included a review of research on friendship that portrays anything but excess candor: "Friends do not disclose their true opinion of each other (Felson, 1993). Friends avoid judging each other (Goffman, 1959). Friends discuss each other's positive rather than negative traits (Blumberg, 1972). Friends are eager to report good but not bad news (Tesser & Rosen, 1975)."

Does this make Pat a bad friend? No, but it does hint at room for improvement.

The study Campbell, Sedikides, Reeder and Elliot did was designed to see whether pairs of friends would try to screw each other out of credit for doing well on a joint test or blame each other for doing badly. The scientific name for what the four intrepid researchers were studying is actually pretty good as these things go—the Self-Serving Bias, or SSB. The researchers wanted to compare how big a factor SSB would be between friends as opposed to pairs of strangers.

So they rounded up 152 undergraduate students at the University of North Carolina, Chapel Hill. Half of them signed up in pairs as friends and the other half signed up in time slots with a partner they did not know. Apparently, word had gotten around about Leon and Jimbo, those cheapskate researchers back in chapter 13 who paid students money to be in a study and then took it back at the end. So these experimenters had to pay their volunteers with extra credit toward their grades in psych courses.

After subjects showed up for the test, they were paired off either as friends or as pairs of strangers. Then they were put in different rooms, one to a room, where the researchers gave them a test of "creativity." Asking college students to name as many different uses as they can for a brick and a candle is begging for abuse, but the researchers did it anyway. Because it would be no fun at all not to trick the poor test subjects in some way, the experimenters conspired not to tell the test pairs their true joint scores on the creativity task. Instead, they were given fabricated combined scores that had no relation to how their pair actually performed.

When the undergrads had run out of creative uses for a candle, they were interviewed, one by one. They were told that their scores had been combined with those of the person in the other room—either a friend or a stranger. Regardless of how the pair members actually did on their own, some pairs were told they and their partner together scored low (in the 31st percentile) and that their performance sucked. The other half of the subjects were told their pair scored high (in the 93rd percentile) and they were brilliant.

At this point, one or both people in twelve of the pairs guessed they were being duped, and their reward was that they were thrown out of the study. They, the truly brilliant ones, went on to investigate X-files for the FBI.

The experimenters then asked the 128 gullible souls who remained two questions, assuring them that their partner would never be told their answer:

1. On a scale of 1 to 10, who was most responsible for the outcome of this test?
2. On a scale of 1 to 10, who made the greatest *positive* contribution to this test?

These two diabolical questions are how the experimenters set the test subjects up to see if they would blame each other for the low score or take all the credit for the high score, respectively, and whether they'd do differently if the subject in the other room was a pal versus a stranger. You'll be pleased to know that friends didn't steal credit from friends or cast blame on them. But if the other subject in your pair was a stranger, you stiffed him royal, proving that, while as individuals we can be pretty selfish, friends don't give friends the shaft.

This heartwarming research is all about the loyalty of friends. Far from demanding total honesty, this loyalty requires that we do not hurt our friends, no matter how easy and obvious the opportunity. So the next time you help your friend who could lose a few pounds zip up her dress, zip your lip, too.

33

THE WINNER'S CUP

To be fair to Patrick, though he is often too candid with SpongeBob, he does love his pal. When Sponge abandons Bikini Bottom to live the more "natural" life of his beloved jellyfish, Patrick is so devastated he tries to physically capture Sponge and bring him back home. Patrick, sticking up for SpongeBob when Neptune is dissing him, takes repeated bolts of lightning and ends up with his face on his butt, but still he won't stop. He beats himself silly trying to help Sponge get into that bad-boy bar, the Salty Spittoon.

Part of what draws Patrick to SpongeBob is admiration. Sponge does so many things well. Everyone likes him. Patrick wishes he could be like that.

And therein lies a certain danger.

One morning, the pink starfish is dozing against the

stone wall of his house when he's awakened by a package stuffed in his mouth. When he unwraps it, he is overjoyed to find an award—a nice gold cup, suitable for his mantel. He rushes to show it off to SpongeBob, only to find that the award cup was actually meant for Sponge. The mailfish delivered it to the wrong mouth.

Pat is glum. Sponge suggests they go for ice cream and, in the diabolical chaining of events that drives all the best cartoons, where should Pat rush to get the ice cream but to Sponge's closet. When he pulls the door open, a tidal wave of SpongeBob's other trophy cups inundates him.

I'll never win an award, Pat wails.

Pop quiz: The correct thing for SpongeBob to say at this point is:

A. "We can't all be geniuses, Pat."

B. "Just look at this mess you made."

C. "Sure you can win an award. I'll help you."

(*Jeopardy!* theme music plays while we think about this.) While we puzzle over the correct answer (please stop waving your hands and put your arms down, everyone), let's take time out to consider what is happening here. Patrick is pleased to get the award, so pleased he doesn't bother to read the inscription on the plaque. He rushes at once to show it off to his best friend. Was the thinking here, "I got an award, and I know you love me so much you'll be overjoyed," or, "I got an award and you didn't"? The second might explain why Pat got so bummed after he finally accepted that the award givers had not misspelled his name "S-p-o-n-g-e-B-o-b S-q-u-a-r-e-P-a-n-t-s." If he wanted to show Sponge the award to make his friend happy for him, then why wasn't he happy for SpongeBob when it turned out the winner's cup was for him? Why was he figuratively crushed when all the awards fell out of the closet on him?

Envy comes to mind.

For what is surely the most momentous case of envy in the history of the universe, we turn to Lucifer and God. Lucifer loved God and vice versa. The details are sketchy, but all the accounts stress that. God was the leader, of course, but that was fine with Lucifer. . . .

Not.

So Lucifer starts talking trash, gonna be like the Most High, move up in the heavenly hierarchy. Instead, he gets himself thrown out and cast down to guess where. Lucky us. Changes his name to Satan, makes himself into a snake-headed pool cue and shoots Eve smack into Adam. They both drop in the corner pocket, and it's a scratch and we've got death, destruction, sin, disease, and plagues, and on top of that mosquitoes change from nice little insects that cross-pollinate tiny flowers into vicious bloodsuckers that even Hindus slap when no one is looking.

Maybe all Lucifer had in mind was a little friendly competition, but it didn't work out that way.

Obviously, competition can be good—wonderful, even—and not just in sports. Watson and Crick were competing against Linus Pauling, an associate if not a friend, and a lot of other researchers they knew, bearing down hard to be the first to discover the structure of DNA. In the end, we all were the winners. Competition with the Japanese is why we now make better cars in America. Without the Soviet Union, we might never have landed men on the moon, assuming that wasn't all just a fraud perpetrated in some Hollywood studio and the world is really flat. (If it is, the right kind of competition will make it go 'round.)

But as often as not, competition ends badly between friends.

Take Julius Caesar and his friend and eventual phlebotomist, Brutus. The two were as close as potstickers and dip'n sauce right up until Brutus stuck it to Julius in the Forum. Brutus's official reason for helping stab his friend to death was to save Rome, though in fact the assassination threw the country into years of turmoil and handed it over to dictators without half of Julius's charm. Sixteen centuries later, Shakespeare made much of Brutus's nobility in his play *Julius Caesar*, and that version of the man has tended to cling, even though accuracy was hardly the strong suit of a playwright who wasn't even sure how to spell his own name. The fact is, Brutus had a fire in his belly to get ahead. He loaned money to Salamis (the town, not the meat), then charged 48 percent interest and starved five town dignitaries to death to collect. Brutus joined Pompey in a civil war against Caesar, clearly hoping to take his friend down a peg. By the time Pompey had lost the war and the top eight inches of his height, Brutus was back in Caesar's camp. That Julius forgave him shows they truly were friends. But it is just as true that Brutus resented Julius's power and made it his personal mission in life to undercut his more powerful friend whenever he could. That day in the Forum, with Caesar's blood on his hands and an angry mob looking for someone to punish, what was Brutus gonna say? "I just got sick of Julius lording it over me"?

Envy can be tough on friendships, even when there's no stabbing involved. SpongeBob weathers the shoals of Patrick's jealousy with great skill and patience. When he tries to help Patrick win a prize, the reward he gets is that Patrick starts copying everything he does, from his clothes to what he says and the expressions on his face, until even the sweet-natured Sponge is seriously annoyed. He could have bagged the whole thing right there, but instead he hangs in there with Patrick and takes advantage of none of the many opportunities to tell him what an idiot he's being, and in the end, Patrick earns his own unique award—in a way it would be wrong to give away here.

It wasn't the only time Sponge had to deal with Patrick's envy. When the annual fry cook competition rolled around, Patrick wanted to compete, too. Patrick was offended when SpongeBob gently pointed out that he wasn't a fry cook. In turn, he offends SpongeBob by saying, "How hard could it be?"

Pat gets Plankton to hire him at the Chum Bucket so he can compete in the games and go head-to-head with his best buddy in the wrestling ring. It gets pretty intense there for a while, but they find their way back to friendship in a way we shall leave out of this book, because there's already been enough foolishness about Patrick and SpongeBob liking each other a little too much. They don't. All right?

"Not"—to quote Jerry and George—"that there's anything wrong with that."

Bottom line: Next time you're tempted to get in the ring with your best buddy, or challenge your girlfriend to see which one of you can get the cute guy in Accounting, or start asking each other what your IQs are, which inevitably leads to grief, remember a simple rule. Unless you intend to discover the cure for the common cold, a little competition with your friends goes a long way, and going too far is too near.

Oh yes, and the correct answer is C.

GETTING ALONG WITH YOURSELF

34

BEING YOURSELF

Woody Allen once confessed, "My only regret in life is that I'm not someone else." Woody does sort of look like a lost son of Alan Greenspan, but that's probably not what he meant.

Every mortician can repeat from memory the line people often say as they file past the coffin of a dear departed: "Don't he look like himself?" (Every competent mortician, anyway.)

Second only to those guys with big hats who guard the queen of England, morticians are the world champions at keeping a straight face, and it's a good thing. Who else would our friends and relatives at the funeral expect us to look like? No matter how we might try to copy another person, as Patrick did SpongeBob, we will still and forever be ourselves.

But what, exactly, does that mean?

For thousands of years people lived and died without giv-

ing the idea of a "self" much thought. Our caveman friends Ig and Og were too busy chasing down food and staying warm to ponder the nature of their own consciousness. Ig, using internal grunts for thought, might have wondered how come when his neighbor Og stared at Ig's mate and winked at her and gyrated his hips, Ig got this pressure in his head like when he hit his thumb with a rock trying to shave a new spear point.

Or maybe Ig just went over and hit Og with a stick without being aware of his "self" having any particular thoughts or insights. We just don't know.

Eventually, as the story goes, the cave people developed language and moved into houses with toilets and running water, and carried around silver coins with which they could buy food instead of having to go out and chase it down themselves. More and more people started having time to consider concepts other than survival. Some of them decided to think more about what made them tick, and thus was the philosopher class born.

Philosophers sat around for several more millennia like Rodin's sculpture *The Thinker*, staring at the ground or off into space, musing about our internal makeup. At first, they didn't get very far with it. For example, after much thought and observation, Aristotle proclaimed that the primary purpose of the brain was to produce snot. A perfectly logical conclusion for its time, and valuable evidence that the common cold has been around at least since 400 BC.

Hippocrates got a little further by shrewdly observing that blows to the head caused unconsciousness. It is not clear whether he conducted experiments on this or merely observed chance occurrences.

To cut to the chase, we now have psychologists and neurologists and psychiatrists and casino operators, all of whom are dedicated to understanding the intricacies of the individual human brain and psyche. While by no means are all students of mental makeup introverts, the introverted mind is particularly prone to examine itself.

But is it *useful* to sit around pondering ourselves?

To help answer this obvious trick question, let's look at some examples from *SpongeBob SquarePants*. Sponge doesn't seem to spend much time thinking about his inner self. He just goes out there and lives according to his principles of kindness, staying "ready," and being a gregarious showboat. But one night, while lying on his triple mattress sound asleep, SpongeBob dreams, and in his dream becomes as self-conscious as we have ever seen him. He starts by wondering if the SpongeBob he can now see lying asleep in his bed is him, or whether this suddenly separate entity he now seems to be is the "real" him. A deep question, but he loses interest in it almost at once. After dreaming he's driving, only to have his license yanked by Mrs. Puff, Sponge does something very typical for his extroverted self. He goes around the peaceful nightscape of Bikini Bottom visiting the dreams of his friends. Popping in on the sleeping activities of Gary, Patrick, Mr. Krabs, Pearl, Sandy, and Squidward, SpongeBob serves as a lens to magnify the inner selves of each friend for us.

The most surprising dream is Gary's, in which we see that the unassuming pet snail is, in his sleep, quite another creature entirely. Of all the dreams Sponge snoops around in that night, Squidward's is the most complex, in keeping with Squid's elaborately neurotic inner self. In his dream, Squid is playing his clarinet on the concert stage, serenading a fish king and his dignitaries. To Squidward's dismay, SpongeBob cannot simply observe but sidles in at the king's elbow and whispers distracting jokes to his highness. Joining Squid onstage, Sponge tries to help his faltering performance but instead causes an adoring stampede to himself, which knocks Squid into a fruit stand situated, with impeccable dream logic, in an aisle of the concert hall.

Playing a shrink, you have no doubt observed that Squid's dream expresses an ambitious need for accomplishment not present in the sleeping fantasies of SpongeBob's other friends. It reflects the longings of Squidward's waking life, as seen in other episodes. When Squid looks in a mirror, he sees an artist, a musician, a cephalopod of high accomplishment. On the three-dimensional side of the glass, he rarely measures up to that image. For example, he signs up to teach an art class, but only one pupil shows up, and of course it would be SpongeBob. An eager student, Sponge soon demonstrates more talent in his little finger than Squid could muster in all six limbs. That the untutored fry cook should be so gifted drives Squid nuts.

In the talent show Squid organizes for Mr. Krabs to bring more customers to the Krusty Krab, the crowd spurns Squid's interpretive dance routine but raves when the curtain accidentally parts to show SpongeBob mopping the stage—the only gig Squidward would allow him that night. Once again, fate decrees that the effortless extrovert will best the striving introvert. Anyone who watches this episode would probably agree that Squid's dance act is actually quite good. Maybe the right question isn't why the crowd rejects Squidward's well-rehearsed production and applauds SpongeBob just for showing up, but why this has to matter so much to the infuriated Squid.

35

SEEING YOURSELF

Maybe what Squid needs to do is stop trying to impress a crowd and try harder to be the sort of squid he himself can respect.

To do this, he must first take a good, hard look at the self he is now.

Easy to say, hard to do. Heisenberg is famous for pointing out that we can't measure something without becoming a distorting part of what we are measuring. This principle demonstrates itself in each dream SpongeBob "observed," and would have occurred even had he tried simply to watch his own dream. Imagine we can shine a flashlight around inside our mind. The beam is our focus of attention. When we try to turn that beam on our truest "self," some of the things we might most need to illuminate are gonna see the beam coming and elude it, staying in the dark.

That's why shrinks like to hear about your dreams. It isn't just because they are professional voyeurs of the soul. It's because a dream is the flashlight shining itself around, with no conscious hand to guide it. In his waking fantasies, Squidward could see himself pleasing the king and his court. In his dreams, he sees someone spoiling it—*and it's never his fault*.

If, when he awakens, Squid could take hold of that flashlight and shine it deeper, illuminating parts of himself he won't normally look at, maybe he could see in its true light the sarcastic and sour attitude he brings to the world, which he wrongly takes for cleverness. If he could look into his insides and see what other people see on his outside, he'd have the information he needs to get why people are more receptive to SpongeBob than to him. That would be step one in changing himself into a squid he could respect, and thereby building a happier life.

Why doesn't Squidward see his own hand in his failures?

We all know he's not alone. Practically everyone in the world except for us has trouble seeing what they're doing wrong. We take a good hard look at ourselves on a regular basis and, well, we aren't doing anything wrong. But everyone else could sure use a tune-up.

Shrinks have a name for this self-perceived perfection of ours. They call it defensiveness. It starts at birth. When we're infants, anything goes. We want to cry, we cry. We want to spit up milk, we spit it up. When it's nap time, we nod off in people's faces with no thought of it being rude. We peed on Uncle Milo's face that one time Mom got him to change our diaper. No fear of consequences, no worries.

Sooner or later, the parental units in our lives, those awesome towering gods who lean down to pick us up, decide we've had a free ride long enough. They start telling and showing us right from wrong. Eve got to eat a forbidden apple and be done with it, but our knowledge of good and evil comes over a long, attritive campaign that is well on its way by the time we're two. We get into the cupboard at Auntie's house and are digging her strawberry jam from the jar with our fingers and trying to hit our mouths with it, and in comes our Aunt Mozelle, and we say, "My mommy says dis jam is good for me."

We have just been defensive. We know we're doing something wrong, but instead of giving Auntie a sheepish grin and saying, "Busted," we come up with an alibi, just like that, in a split second. Two years old, and already it's not our fault.

By the time we're teenagers, we have become experts in our own defense. Instead of admitting we shouldn't have taken the station wagon and driven out on the pond and done donuts on the ice, we shift the grounds of the argument: "You never let me do *anything*. How come it's *your* car? I thought we were a family and it was the *family* car. How was I supposed to know the ice would break?"

The sad irony of defense mechanisms is that we build them to keep the pain of others' disapproval out, but instead they keep us from seeing what we need to know to master ourselves and our situation. It's natural to want to think we're perfect. But here's the news flash: If you're willing to give that up, your reward will be that, each time you find out you were wrong, you will gain more power and control over your situation. After all, if something is your fault, you have the power to change it and control the situation. If it's someone else's fault, you don't have control, and you just gotta hope. So to see and admit when we're in the wrong isn't just wise; it's powerful.

The alternative is to go on denying—and arguing. If the biggest cost of defensiveness is that we're not changing when we need to, the second biggest is all the time and energy we waste arguing. No one likes arguers. That's why there's all those lawyer jokes. Lawyers argue for a living. You say toe-*may*-toe, they'll say toe-*mah*-toe. It's their love of arguing about how many angels can dance on the head of a pin that annoys us.

On the other hand, when the police arrest you for walking out with two cases of cat food without paying, and you simply forgot to go through the checkout because you were wondering if that gassy feeling you get every night after eating pizza is cancer of the bowel, but now they've taken you to jail, and you're technically guilty but innocent of any illegal intent, and they confiscated your belt and shoelaces, and you're afraid to take a shower, who do you want in your corner? A comedian with the best lawyer jokes, or a lawyer?

But if you are not a lawyer, and you find yourself arguing a lot, unless you've got a two-year-old or a teenager it's a warning sign you're too defensive—or in lay terms, too unwilling or even unable to be wrong. Here's a simple reality

test. First, we agree that no one is right all the time. Next, we admit that, like everyone else, some of the time, we could be wrong. So far, so good. But we aren't even halfway there, because the real rub is in letting yourself be wrong this time. If you find that you must always win the argument you're in, just the one you're in, and not all the others, then you are actually saying you can never be wrong, because last time and next time never come. Only "this time" exists, and if you can never be wrong now, you can never be wrong.

The key to lowering that defensive barrier is not to view it as looking to see if you're wrong. Instead, think of it as seeing if there's anything you can find and change in yourself that will give you more power. You'll have a nasty little stab of fear about losing face if you admit you were wrong. Ignore it. Think instead of how you felt about the last person who admitted to you that he was wrong. You liked him better, right? You thought, "What a reasonable person this is. He's not afraid to admit he's wrong."

If you're right, you're right. But if you're right all the time, you're lying to yourself and you need to look for that chance to get smarter, then feel the power.

36

iZZY AND DUZZY

Popeye, a cartoon character from a bygone era, expressed the prevailing sentiment of his time when he proclaimed, "I yam what I yam." There was no *Psychology Today* on the newsstand back when Popeye first strode onto the scene, arms swinging; no Montel Williams or Jerry Springer delving into the wounded psyches of sisters battling over the same potbellied, slack-jawed male who had slept with all of them. Popeye reflected the moral certainty of the times.

Then the late sixties and seventies ushered in the era of pop psychology, and with it the concept of the adjustable brain. This wonderful gizmo was invented by the Monty Python comedy troupe—a mechanical, hatlike device that sat on top of the head, thus being easier to service than the brain it replaced. The Monty Python brain did require occasional tinkering when those who wore it started spouting gibberish, but a few turns of a screwdriver or a blow from a hammer were often enough. Alas, these Monty Python brains are in very short supply today and almost impossible to find, and even if you could find one, the repair technicians have all gone on to other things.

Which means we'll have to tinker with our own brains.

When we go in, what are we looking for?

A good start would be our ideal self—the self Mr. Krabs should have consulted before he gave his daughter, Pearl, a pair of rubber boots for her birthday. The sole factor in his choice of the boots was that they were cheap. This is not because he didn't love his daughter, but because Mr. Krabs himself is cheap, cheap, cheap. He let this cheapness elbow aside his better self.

Pearl, possibly having read somewhere that gifts are in the eye of the beholder, wailed as only a whale can and rejected the gift, instead of slipping off, as she should have done, and quietly returning the boots to Bikini Bottom's Salvation Navy. This left Mr. Krabs stuck with a nerdy, useless pair of boots. Once again, without checking himself for any ideals he might possess, he could think only of recouping the two bucks he spent for the boots. So when SpongeBob comes in for work, Krabs spins this tale of the boots being very special and belonging to the greatest fry cook ever, and sure enough, an awed and gullible Sponge takes them off his hands, overpaying so lavishly even Mr. Krabs feels a prick of guilt.

Just a prick, not enough to turn Sponge down; just enough to suggest that somewhere inside Krabs might lurk the ghost of an ideal or two.

Chapter 32 (in case you took a shortcut and missed it) introduced us to the Self-Serving Bias, a study in which college students were loyal to their friends but stole credit from and dumped blame on partners who were strangers. This tendency to put ourselves first over everyone but true friends is present in most of us. The SSB probably had some original survival value, dating back to the time when there was often only one drumstick to feed ten cavemen, and the altruists of that time, such as they might have been, starved to death from unselfishness before they could breed.

However Self-Serving Bias came about, what we need to do now is realize its heyday has passed. Times have changed. Restaurants and grocery stores throw away food. We pay our farmers not to grow the stuff. While these amazing conditions do not—sadly—apply all over the world, if you have enough time and inclination to read this book, it is a happy reality of your life that you need not make the guy next to you starve so that you can live to breed. If we bring our Self-Serving Bias to heel, society will work better and that will be good for all of us.

When we look into ourselves for something to admire, a conscience would be high on the list. Mr. Krabs's needs work. He feels guilty about selling the boots to SpongeBob, but that guilt doesn't do the actual injured party any good. All it does is punish Krabs. Oddly enough, as a result, Krabs might actually find it easier to screw SpongeBob over the next chance he gets. If Mr. Krabs believes he has been punished for what he did to SpongeBob, then he may feel that's the end of it. "I cheated him, yes, but I paid for it. The account is square."

Not really.

Once again, the difference between "are" and "do" has reared its head in our narrative. Mr. Krabs *feels* guilty. Mr. Krabs *does* nothing to banish that guilt; he simply experiences it and feels punished by it. Mr. Krabs is an "Izzy"— the "is" trumps the "does" in his life, and no restitution is made to the victim.

Krabs would respect himself more, and thus be happier with himself, if he could make himself a "Duzzy." To find out how to do this, read on.

37

BEING BRAD PITT

Let's return for a moment to chapter 34—to Woody Allen's regret that he isn't someone else. It is perfectly true that he cannot be, and neither can we. From the moment we enter this world, we are unique, even if an identical twin plops out right behind us. The twin would have your genes and your cells, but the minute you both are born she has already been the one on the left for several months, and you've been the one on the right, and if Mom always slept on her right side, you're already different from Sis. You have been, even from that moment before birth, and always will be, uniquely you. Nothing you do can ever change that.

That is the sense in which Popeye was right when he said, "I yam what I yam."

The sense in which he was wrong is in how little credit

he's giving himself for how much he could change what that yam is. He could make it into sweet potato pie or bake it and put butter in the middle. Or he could throw it in a food fight. The possibilities are nearly endless. Popeye could not stop being the collection of brain, body, and animation cells that make him different from everyone else. But were he human—or had he a different cartoonist—he could stop being a sailor man and go army. He could jilt the dithery Olive Oyl for confident Betty Boop. He could grow his hair long, start eating broccoli instead of spinach, and see a plastic surgeon about forearm reduction.

Maybe he shouldn't do these things, maybe he wouldn't want to, but he could.

Or he could stop beating up poor Bluto and reason with him, or learn to avoid unnecessary conflict in the first place. He wouldn't be nearly so funny, but that's our problem. He might be happier and feel better about himself.

Woody Allen can't be Alan Greenspan's son, even if he wanted to, but he can be a different Woody Allen, and he has been, every time he acted in a movie. . . .

All right, bad example. Woody Allen always plays himself. Dustin Hoffman, then.

The "Ben" of *The Graduate* is not the CDC biologist we saw in *Outbreak* or the shrink we watched in *Sphere*. The impassioned lawyer of *Runaway Jury* has little in common with the twitchy crime boss in *Confidence*.

But Hoffman's an actor, you say. He has a real life behind all that. Yes, and you'd better believe that real life has been affected and changed and shaped by all the roles he's played. Remember our axiom from chapter 13: It's easier to act yourself into a new way of feeling than to feel yourself into a new way of acting. This axiom has a first cousin: It's better to *act* yourself into a new way of being than to feel you *are* that person when you're not.

Of course, acting like a different you works best if the particular new you that you have in mind is someone you have a decent chance of becoming.

SpongeBob is worried when a couple of nerdy customers drinking sodas at the Weenie Hut Jr. treat him as one of their own. The robot bartender scans him and solemnly agrees he is a weenie, and that really sets Sponge off. He decides he'll prove he's not a weenie by getting himself admitted to the Salty Spittoon, which only accepts tough guys. The minute SpongeBob steps into a line of muscular, grizzled sea creatures waiting to get past the bouncer, it's obvious he doesn't belong. But the stinging observations of a couple of weenies have provoked him into trying to be something he is physically and constitutionally unable to be.

In another episode the absorbent one demonstrates that you must be careful whom you emulate. At a convention, Sponge spots his hero Kevin, one of the world's greatest jelly-fishers. SpongeBob adores Kevin. He'd like nothing better (he believes) than to be like him. Attaching himself to the sea cucumber's retinue, Sponge soon becomes the victim of a number of cruel tricks his hero plays on him. Slowly, it sinks in that Kevin isn't very nice, and that he's really not worth emulating.

You will avoid this lesson if you choose your heroes with care. You are not trying to become the person you admire, but to become a new you who shares these effective characteristics. To do this, you observe the things your model says and does that attract you. If you admire these behaviors in someone else, you'll admire them in yourself, and that's what this chapter is all about—getting along better with yourself. The best way to do this is to be that elusive "self" we can respect.

Isn't it fakey, you ask, to copy someone else?

If it is, we're all in trouble, because that's how we learn how to act in the first place when we're kids and then teenagers. We don't decide how tall we're gonna be, or what color eyes we'll have, or where and to whom we're born. But we do decide how we're gonna act in this world, and we do a great deal of that when we're young by observing others. As kids, we might realize we're doing this or we might not, but observe and copy we will. Indeed, to ignore the good and bad behavior we see around us is a mistake. If our attitude is that people can just like us for what we are, and we've done nothing to shape ourselves into a likeable person, we'll get exactly what we deserve. As we have already seen, "are" is passive. It's status quo. And worst of all, what we think we "are" doesn't have much relationship to how other people see us—unless we work to make it so. So it's best to get ourselves organized and give some serious attention to what we see in others that seems to work well in this world.

The potential model for how to act can be your best friend, your significant other, Jesus, Gandhi, or the character in a novel. Think about why you like them. What is it they do that's so nice? Do they remember to compliment others when they've done well? Do they listen more than they speak? Do they talk about others more than themselves? These are all things we might see and copy from the repertoire of human behaviors to make our already wonderful selves even more wonderful, not just to the people around us, but to ourselves.

Maybe you really are fine just the way you are. Some people are.

But if you sometimes wake up in the middle of the night and wonder why you're always having to argue with people, or you flash back to the party last weekend where you talked about yourself all night, tried to get yourself out there so people would like you, and instead people kept moving away, and one woman actually pretended she was pregnant and had to rush herself to the hospital, well then, your brain is giving you a brief window of opportunity. You can tell yourself, "I'm fine," roll over, and send that worm of doubt back to your unconscious mind where it can safely go on causing you misery. Or you can take a good look inside, and another good look around you, and become someone you can like and respect.

MASTERING THE UNIVERSE

THE 10TH WAY

38

ELEVEN MINUTES

Squidward has just landed in the kelp jungle and realizes he's lost in the wilderness with SpongeBob and Patrick. Though in his heart he hides a soft spot for the two, Squid prefers to act like they are beneath him, simpletons, silly and annoying. Now, marooned with these two ruthlessly cheery gomers, Squidward wails, "Why must every eleven minutes of my life be filled with misery?"

Squid has just had what we call an existential moment, and his breakthrough insight is not that there is misery in this world. We learn that the minute the masked giant who pulls us from the primal warmth smacks our ass. Somehow, Squidward has sensed a less obvious truth of his existence—that he lives life in chunks exactly equal to an episode in a cartoon show.

What will he do with this information?

What *can* he do?

Ernesto Spinelli, in his book *The Interpreted World—An Introduction to Phenomenological Psychology*, says that the aim of existential psychotherapy is "to offer the means for individuals to examine, confront and clarify and reassess their understanding of life, the problems encountered throughout their life, and the limits imposed upon the possibilities inherent in being-in-the-world."

In English, to squeeze more happiness out of life, we need to study what life is.

Life is what the existential philosophers prefer to call existence. Not just because existence has more syllables but because the term "existence," the way they mean it, is broader than "life." Life is just you going around being alive. Existence is the "around" as well—not just you, but the universe in which you live, and not just the universe as it is, but the universe as you think it is.

To illustrate the difference, let's imagine we go into the lion house at the zoo (the kings of beasts are indoors in their cages today because it's too cold to be outdoors). We walk down the row of cages admiring the beautiful lions and lionesses up close. How strong they are. How big their teeth are when they yawn. Aren't they beautiful?

We make a face at the biggest male lion. In the deluded belief it will impress our girlfriend, we turn and wag our butt at the big brute.

And then we suddenly realize that the door of his cage is unlocked. All the lion would have to do is rub against it and it would swing open.

We impress our girlfriend with how fast we can run.

Then, ashamed, we run back, sling her over our shoulder and run out again.

But the cage wasn't really unlocked, it just looked that way.

Every bit of our behavior was based on a combination of our own nature and what we thought the reality of the situation was. We went from amusement to terror to shame, and finally to mortification, based at every turn on what we thought and perceived was real. Not what was real, but what we interpreted as real.

Welcome to existence. If we're gonna master the universe, we gotta know as much about it as we can. And then figure out which parts to ignore. If Squidward works on his insight about the eleven minutes, he might decide it's one of those "limits" Spinelli talks about—that his free will is in question, that maybe someone is writing a script for him that he must live out. Thankfully for us, his thinking never gets that far, since he might go into a neurotic tailspin, confine himself to his tiki house and stop doing funny things. Of course, we humans never feel like puppets acting out a script. . . .

Excuse me. Don't know what made me say that.

Remember grade school? That afternoon you sat in your classroom, your fifth-grade teacher Miss Bailey trying to drum basics of English grammar into the mutton heads of you and your classmates? It's 2:12 P.M., and school lets out for the day at 3:00 P.M., and you have sworn to yourself that you will not look at the clock over the door again for at least ten minutes. So you gaze out the tall window beside your desk at the playground sparkling green under a blue sky plied by cumulus ships with billowing sails. The playground swings sway an inch or two in a lazy breeze while the teeter-totter planks sit dead still, canted in eternal indecision. The faint aromas of orange peel and peanut butter on waxed paper linger from lunch, when Jack Cash hung a carrot stick from one nostril and made you laugh and blow milk out your nose. Gazing out the window, you think of your life, laid out by your parents and teachers, stretching away in front of you, three more years before eighth grade graduation, then another four of high school, and then another four of college, and then another four of medical school, and then another four of internship and residency, that's nineteen more years, nine more than you've yet been alive, and then after those nineteen, at the ancient age of twenty-nine, you will be free to have recess all you want, and you forget and look at the clock and it is 2:14 P.M., and a groan seizes deep in your lungs.

You didn't think of those nineteen years as a script, maybe, but it was, and you played your appointed role and now here you are, and you're freer in some ways than you were then, but still not free.

At least Squidward gets a break every eleven minutes.

You're only in fifth grade, but you're starting to get that time is relative. A couple of minutes can be long or short. It depends on what's going on or not going on around you. Ten years old, and you have discovered something important about the universe.

39

FEAR OF FLOATING

Here are four other things that are important to know about existence:

1. To fully understand the nature of it is impossible. However . . .
2. Giving existence no thought leaves you with squat preparation for its twists and turns.
3. Drawing the wrong conclusions about existence can make life worse, not better.
4. Having the right handle on existence will make your life happier.

So what *is* existence really like?
Denizens of Bikini Bottom might well ask themselves,

"How come if I'm a fish, I walk on two legs?" Or, "Why am I drinking this glass of water when I'm surrounded by water?" These questions would require a higher consciousness of existence than most characters in Bikini Bottom seem to have. The fish "extras" show no awareness that legs on a fish happen only in evolution textbooks.

But Bikini Bottom still presents plenty of existential dilemmas.

SpongeBob and Patrick would like to buy a balloon, but they have no money. Earlier in the eleven minutes, when Sponge asked Mr. Krabs about some of his stuff that looks like stolen goods (such as Plankton's tiny lawnmower and some hair curlers), a sweaty and defensive Mr. Krabs insisted he only borrowed them—that you can borrow anything so long as you return it before it's missed. So now Sponge and Pat decide they will "borrow" the balloon. When the vendor is looking the other way, they snatch it and off they go.

They haven't borrowed it for sixty seconds before the balloon pops.

A quirk in the nature of balloons, which they didn't think hard enough about beforehand, has just changed the lives of SpongeBob and Patrick. Their soothing fiction that they are only borrowing the balloon has exploded with the thing itself. They can no longer return it. They are now thieves. The same act they deluded themselves into thinking was okay only a minute ago they now must face as not being okay. Such are the shifting sands of reality.

As criminals, they have two choices: they can turn themselves in or escape, leaving their town and homes behind forever, living a life of crime on the road. Again neglecting to weigh any of the existential complications, they run away. Far from Bikini Bottom, they sit around a fire and mourn all they've lost. SpongeBob, even now the optimist, points out that at least they have this nice campfire to keep them warm. Perversely, Patrick chooses that moment to wonder, "Hey, if we're underwater—"

And the fire winks out.

This type of existential moment happens in all of our lives.

Say you are an introvert, and leery of bodies of water because (unbeknownst to you) Mom tried to drown you in your bassinet when you were a baby. But you're in the Caribbean and you've been reading on the beach for days, a novel about Navy SEALs doing all this exciting underwater stuff, and you've always fantasized about snorkeling, and five days sitting on the beach while everyone else goes in the water is starting to wear thin. By George, you're going for it. So you get your hotel mask and fins on, and slither off the resort's boat into forty feet of warm, crystal-clear water. Below you, parrot fish and sergeant majors and trumpets and squirrels (sans Sandy's air helmet) drift over colorful fan and brain coral. You are floating, weightless, all the mahimahi and pork you've been stuffing into your pie hole at the luaus lifted from your bones by the buoyant sea. Wow, this is fun.

And then you think, "I sure hope my mask doesn't start to leak."

Suddenly, the fact that you are in forty feet of water strikes you as scary instead of neat. An image of your dead body rolling along the bottom flashes through your mind. You lift your head for a reassuring glance at the boat and, instead of being where you left it, it's now a tiny speck bobbing on the horizon. All warmth evaporates from your body. You lower your head and take three determined strokes toward the boat, then notice that a piece of brain coral below you, instead of moving down your body, is actually drawing farther away from your head. Dear God, you're being pulled backward, away from the boat. *You're caught in a riptide! You'll never get to the boat, everyone knows you can't swim against a current, you could drown—*

Your snorkel is making these raspy puffing noises. Thought has all but fled. It doesn't occur to you simply to roll onto your back and float to shore, which is much closer than the boat. You are swimming for the boat, swimming for the boat with everything you have.

And what do you know, you get there, because you were only in the gentle current for about three seconds and you sideslipped out without knowing it. Heart banging, you clamber into the boat, where some of the other hotel guests are sitting on the gunwales, including a cute chick, so you drawl, "Sure is great out there today." They all look at you with concern, and a woman touches your shoulder—not the cute chick but the one who looks like Aunt Bea—and you realize fear has blanched your skin as white as toothpaste.

All this because you had a sudden ill-advised thought. Unlike the experience at the lion cage, a large part of this existential crisis came from the past you were too young to record in a way you could remember. Mom didn't really try to drown you in the bassinet, your head just slipped under the water for a second, and she jerked you right out and held you while you cried and coughed your little lungs out. All these years later, that experience, still salted away in there even though you can't remember it, triggered the thought that distorted your existence of that moment from a safe and joyful pleasure to near panic. Had you let go of that last thread of sanity, you could, in fact, have died, and then gone around as a really pissed-off ghost, feeling stupid for all eternity, because nothing short of panic or a satellite falling out of the sky could have killed you in such waters.

If you are an extrovert, such a moment might come to you when you are scuba diving with sharks. You've had a fair amount of experience at this, and you're confident you know how close you can get without causing the shark to bite your head off and leave a really disgusting corpse. For a while, it was enough to be in the vicinity of sharks, then, to get the same thrill, you needed to get a little closer, and a little closer, and now you're thinking of grabbing the tail fin of an eight-foot tiger.

Think again.

Misperception of the universe or your own abilities in it can, in extreme cases, cost you your life. More often it simply screws it up in ways large or small. For SpongeBob and Patrick (as for Squidward when he noticed the eleven-minute thing), the insight that they had a fire going underwater gets lost in the press of their lives. Maybe the information was just too stunning to absorb, like the time you woke up in the middle of the night and thought you saw the scaly green hind leg of an alien exiting your bedroom door, then decided it was only a dream.

It was.

Probably.

In any case, as with many episodes of life in Bikini Bottom, a final twist awaits criminals SpongeBob and Patrick that will recast everything that has happened from the moment they snatched the balloon into yet another light, this time the true one. Had they seen reality as it truly was in the beginning, they'd have saved themselves a great deal of hysteria.

40

WE'RE NOT UGLY, WE STINK

Planet of the Apes (the 1968 original, not the sucky remake) was surely one of the most existential movies ever made for a big commercial audience (as opposed to art films, which routinely immerse us to our pituitaries in existential nuance). *Planet of the Apes*, starring Charlton "Moses" Heston, captured as well as any movie could the extraordinary novel by Pierre Boulle. If you've been on another planet or have declined to rent the DVD because it isn't "serious" enough, well la-de-da, give it a chance. Heston at his mature prime plays an astronaut named Taylor. He and two fellow astronauts land on a planet much like Earth, but in which the apes rule and man is a beast given less credit for intelligence than we currently give our own great apes. As Taylor, mute from a throat wound, tries to persuade the orangutan philosophers and the gorilla generals and the chimpanzee scientists that he is, indeed, intelligent, he must struggle to adapt to a world turned upside down from his own. The inability of all but the freest-thinking apes to accept that he's not a mere animal is an equal challenge to them. This existential double frame of the film is perfectly captured in a comic moment near the end, when Taylor has secured his freedom and, in an impulsive moment, offers a good-bye kiss to Dr. Zira, the female chimp that championed his cause. The smug patronization with which the handsome Heston plays the scene makes it perfect when chimpanzee Dr. Zira hesitates and then apologizes. "It's just that you're so damn ugly." When that line was uttered, all the straight women and gay men in the theater, who'd had nearly a hundred and ten minutes to feast on rugged, handsome Heston striking noble poses and wrestling gorillas in a loincloth, had an existential moment of their own, whether they knew it or not.

To take it a layer deeper, Dr. Zira may have found Taylor ugly, but actress Kim Hunter, the woman inside the chimpanzee suit, almost surely felt otherwise. The movie audience did not see or think of this because their attention was riveted to the surface—the chimp, not the unseen woman beneath who had also played opposite another hunk, Marlon Brando, in *A Streetcar Named Desire*.

This is our life, our universe, presenting many faces, a host of often conflicting "realities," and the ones we perceive, the ones we act upon, will determine our outcomes, not any underlying reality we have missed. You snooze, you lose.

One fine Sunday morning, SpongeBob heads for the kitchen to make his usual weekend snack and finds the cupboard nearly bare. Undaunted, the creative fry cook throws together ketchup, peanuts, onions, and other smelly leftovers from his kitchen. He gulps it down and puts what's left in his pocket, then heads out to tour Bikini Bottom on his day off. Everyone he meets recoils from him with expressions of torment and disgust. Sponge becomes more and more mystified. Patrick joins him and, seeing all the repugnance SpongeBob is eliciting, suggests that maybe it's because SpongeBob is ugly.

At first Sponge laughs this off, but when a fish couple he bids hello turns belly-up and floats toward the surface, he can no longer avoid the "truth." He *is* ugly.

This is when we learn SpongeBob has a pipe organ in his house.

Depressed, he slinks home to hide from the world. Various episodes of *SpongeBob* reveal an amazing inner space to Sponge's pineapple home, including vast libraries, long hallways, and other features that would seem impossible from the modestly sized exterior. But this is just more of the warped existential reality Sponge takes for granted in his world. The problem before him is the geometry not of his space but of his face. He can't bear to think of himself as ugly. He plays horror-movie music on his pipe organ, mopes and broods, while Patrick, ever the helpful friend, tries to comfort him with a story about a barnacle who was so ugly everyone died.

It should be noted at this point that, as a starfish, Patrick not only has no tact, he has no nose, a significant clue to viewers who might have missed the noxious cloud issuing from Sponge's mouth every time he speaks.

SpongeBob is in the midst of an existential crisis. He never lacked for confidence in his looks before and yet, suddenly, he is convinced he is ugly. It changes his whole worldview. Gone is all the brightness, the optimism, the love of being out in the world, mixing it up with people. Why? His appearance has not changed. He looks the same as always.

Because he has wrongly interpreted people's actions, he separates himself and endures the loneliness that is one of the pillars of existential angst. That Sponge is factually wrong is unimportant so long as he believes and acts on his belief.

That guy you like at the office, the one in computer support? You contrive reasons to walk past his cubicle. You always smile and say hello. He glances up and mumbles, "Hi," then returns to his monitor. Bummer. He's really cute, probably has a girlfriend. Or maybe he's gay. Anyway, it's pretty clear you leave him cold.

And then, one day you say "Hi" and pass on by, and something makes you look back, and you catch him standing halfway up in an awkward crouch so he can see over his wall and watch you walk away.

Reality changes.

You get married, have three nerdy but sweet children, and it almost didn't happen because you didn't realize he wasn't gay or disinterested, just shy.

Existential test. You passed. You could just as easily have flunked and your whole life from that time on would have been different. Existence is full of these choices that you will make and make and make whether you know it or not. Be on the lookout. Take a little time to see more clearly and think a little deeper, because we need every edge we can get.

47

APES OF THE DEEP

Clearly, a wrong idea about the universe can mess up your head. Unfortunately, so can a halfway right one that isn't helpful. No episode of *SpongeBob* illustrates this more dramatically than the one where Sponge falls and breaks his butt.

He, Sandy and Patrick are skiing down Sand Mountain on clamshells. Sponge dodges a tree only to trip on a rock and plummet over the edge of a steep drop. The doctor who pieces his busted butt back together with staples and a glue stick warns him to take it easy in the future or he could wind up confined to the Iron Butt.

Taking the doctor's advice to butt, Sponge confines himself to his home. Sandy and Patrick try everything they can think of to lure him back out from the safety of his pineapple castle, but SpongeBob is adamant. The world, he has decided, is a dangerous place. The only way to be sure you won't get hurt is to play it safe and avoid all danger.

We can all remember what we were doing on September 11, 2001. We were at work slamming a second coffee, trying to get our brains started, or at home, flopping back for a peek at the news and weather after getting the kids off to school, or maybe walking around in a chicken suit with front and back boards advertising the new Chick-fil-A restaurant.

Then, bam. The trade towers, the Pentagon, the field in Pennsylvania. Lot of heroes that day. Lot of driving around like maniacs trying to get the kids back, or calling work, or your parents or your children, frantically trying to break through the busy signals. Sad, bad day. Some of us watched the planes hitting the towers, over and over, over and over, until we can see it now without trying, on a dedicated screen in our minds. Bad move, watching that horrible scene so many times, but by the time we figured that out it was too late.

And now it's 2005, and we've spent hundreds of billions on the wars in Iraq and Afghanistan, and on domestic security, all of which are part of the war on terror. Some wins, some losses. Doing what we gotta do—and some of what we don't gotta.

Are we still scared?

Not as bad as we were, but probably more than is good. That extreme extrovert who likes to swim with the sharks didn't like 9/11 any more than the rest of us, but he's not scared and never was. He got out of the water and got his guns and he's over there somewhere in Afghanistan with a beard to his knees, God bless him, hunting Osama bin Laden for fun.

But most of us got scared and stayed pretty scared, and

all it takes to bring it all back is for the head of Homeland Security, God bless him too, to yell, "Condition Orange!"

And when we calm down again, old Osama puts out another tape promising we're all gonna die.

So, for the record, this might not be a bad time to note that we *are* all gonna die, and it didn't take Osama bin Laden to make that true. Everyone ever born on Earth up to the year, let us say, 1870, is dead, with the possible exception of the prophet Elijah, and there's some dispute among Bible scholars about whether he really went straight to heaven in a whirlwind or maybe it was just a metaphor, like "crossing over," or "buying the farm," or "wrong side of the lawn."

Point being, unless some genius comes up with a way to defeat aging, everyone born *after* 1870 will also die. Not to bum ourselves out, but existentially it can be a comforting thought when we use it, as we should, to cut Osama bin Laden and his ilk down to size.

No, no, no, some of you are saying. It isn't just that we'll die *someday*; it's that Osama might, any day now, blow up the city we're living in with a *thermonuclear bomb*!

Maybe. One of those suitcase bombs it would have to be, and that would be really awful if it happened. It might. It could. And if it does, the great majority of us will come through it all right, and the wrath of this country will be terrible to behold. But aren't we forgetting something? Anyone over ten lived through at least a few of the fifty years during which the entire planet could have been destroyed many, many times over by bombs that didn't have to be sneaked into town but that would have rained down from the heavens in a day of apocalypse beyond imagining. The point is not that just because the Cold War didn't result in a nuclear bomb going off, neither will terrorism. It's that we lived with the Cold War and we can live with this. Especially if we let ourselves really live, like we did last time, when the threat was much greater and more horrible. The elders of us will recall we got pretty excited for a while there after Joe Stalin got the A-bomb. Dug us some bomb shelters. Practiced getting under our desks at school. Then we calmed down and enjoyed *Ozzie and Harriet*, and swimming at the beach, Elvis, '59 Cadillacs, and falling in love and laughing, and all the other things that make life worth living.

Constant fear makes life a great deal less worth living.

But if you just can't give it up, well, there're plenty of other things you could decide to be afraid of. Thirty-five thousand Americans die every year from a "bug" called flu, and even if we know that, we still tend to think the worst that can happen with flu is that we'll miss a week of work while we lie in bed *wishing* we could die. It's good that we think that, because, for the most part, it's true. If we ever decide the flu is as dangerous as terrorists, we'll all be going around in those Centers for Disease Control astronaut suits, unable to hold a pencil or shake hands, and afraid to take the helmet off so the doctor can stick that popsicle stick down our throats and look at our tongues.

Speaking of which, recent estimates suggest that doctors and nurses and hospitals may kill as many as 98,000 of us every year with medical errors. They're very sorry and they don't mean to. And we're still a lot better off going to a doctor when we're sick than, say, a certified public accountant.

These days driving accidents kill around forty thousand

people a year—horrible, mangling deaths. When was the last time you felt even a flicker of fear before jumping in your car and taking off? The highway, flu, and medical errors together have caused way more than fifty times as many deaths as the terrorist attacks each and every year since 2001, and yet most of us are not afraid of any of them.

And that's good!

Why are we so afraid of terrorists? Maybe because what they did is so evil. Maybe because we can visualize murder more easily than the rather drawn-out, microscopic ordeal of being killed by a virus. Maybe because the terrorist fearpot gets stirred on a regular basis by any number of well-meaning (and a few not-so-well-meaning) people. The 24/7 news cycle is hungry for anything that'll punch our adrenal glands. Politicians and intelligence officials are afraid we'll blame them if they didn't warn us and warn us and warn us. Hundreds of billions of dollars have a power all their own, and those really big bucks are now gushing into the pockets of people we're paying to keep us from being so afraid. Some of that's necessary, but if the terrorists all crept off tomorrow and blew themselves and each other up, as they so richly deserve, it might take twenty years for the billions to stop pumping, while all along the people who can make us less afraid could have done it for nothing, because they are us.

You want to stock Pellegrino in your basement in case terrorists get to the water supply? Sounds fine. Maybe get some first aid kits, some plastic and duct tape for your windows, if it makes you feel better. Watch out it doesn't make you feel worse, that's all. Remember that inverted "U" of the anxiety/performance curve back under the First Way? Fear is called for now and then, sure, and can give us the edge we might need to avoid unpleasant or dangerous things. Our government should find those terrorists and stop them. But our government, and we, also need to give more thought than we have yet to our national fear and all it contaminates, all it threatens. Too much fear too much of the time will turn us into a nation of willingly enslaved idiots, which would be a shame, because then programs like *Live from Lincoln Center* would have to go off the air and everyone would be playing the tonette and repeating first grade forever.

So, anyway, to get SpongeBob to come out of his house and stop being afraid and playing it safe, finally, Sandy and Patrick concoct a scheme in which Patrick, dressed in a gorilla suit, will pretend to attack Sandy outside SpongeBob's door, and Sponge will have no choice but to rescue his squirrelly friend.

What follows is *Planet of the Apes*, Bikini Bottom–style. It appears that Patrick, in a gorilla suit, is pounding on Sandy, which SpongeBob finds utterly transparent and fake, until Patrick, eating an ice cream cone, wanders up and asks what's happening. Nonplussed, the gorilla who has been pounding on Sandy zips down to reveal Patrick also, now pretty confused by there being two of him. Then the Patrick with the ice cream cone zips down and a "real" gorilla jumps out and starts pounding on both Sandy and Patrick as Sponge watches with growing horror. Of course, the "real" gorilla that is pounding on Sandy and Patrick actually looks to us like a human in a gorilla suit, but that's an entire 'nother layer of existence of which SpongeBob has no knowledge.

Poor Sponge. Reality keeps peeling away like the layers

of an onion to reveal new and deeper realities, and he has to think it all through and decide what's real, and what he can do to help his friends and maybe put his own life back on a better course. Like we'd like to do for ourselves. You have all the information Sponge has. So what do you do about that gorilla out there? Do you head out to confront it, or stay put? If you're gonna beat it, how are you gonna beat it?

By understanding what it really is.

To avoid spoiling it for those who haven't seen the episode, we won't reveal SpongeBob's epiphany here. Suffice it to say that, when the show is over, the camera cuts to a family of actual humans who have been watching the episode and are now scratching their heads and giving each other stunned frowns. The father reaches forward, turns off the set and everything goes to black.

Go figure.

CONCLUSION

For those who'd like more than the two-word summation "Go figure" at the end of the final chapter, this conclusion is for you.

For many of us, "Go figure" has been sapped of its true meaning by its overuse as an expression. Instead of coming across as a simple, imperative sentence, it is often used merely to show puzzlement or amazement. The Boston Red Sox finally win the World Series—go figure. Someone announces that the world is flat after all, and that the moon landing was faked in a studio on "Lot 13." Go figure.

In fact, "Go figure" can also be a way of life, one that can bring us greater happiness. So let's wring all the fuzzy vagueness out of the expression and return it to its rightful state as a life principle. Going and figuring is what SpongeBob and his friends do. They are active, not passive—even Squidward. When SpongeBob decides to become an entrepreneur, he dithers for exactly none of the eleven minutes allotted to this little piece of his life. He simply rustles up some chocolate bars (wholesale, we hope), and tries selling them door to door. Maybe if he'd thought more about it he wouldn't have done it, but the only sure way to know if it would work was to try it. Mr. Krabs decides something is missing at the Krusty Krab, that he's not doing all he could to bring in customers. So he has Squidward organize a talent show and, another time, direct a commercial (until Krabs has to fire Squid for going over budget). In yet another episode, Krabs goes into action himself, building a ramshackle amusement park next to the Krusty Krab during summer vacation, to lure in kids with pockets full of "Munny." None of these schemes work out all that well, but they bring Krabs knowledge he could have gained in no other way. Sandy wonders what it's like on the moon, so she gets herself a rocket and would have gone there had Sponge and Patrick not shanghaied the ship and beaten her to it. Turns out the two buddies can't tell the difference between being on Earth and being on the moon, but what fun they have. Squidward invents "opposite day" in an effort to con SpongeBob and Patrick into being his idea of good neighbors long enough for him to sell his house. The plan self-destructs, but at least Squid had one and acted on it. And when Squidward does manage to sell his house and move into a gated community of other squids, he finds it not to his liking after all, and he returns to his tiki house with a better understanding of what he needs to be happy.

It's "Go figure," not "Figure go," and both verbs are active. The unseen, "understood" part that makes it a sentence is "You." Many of us figure too much and go too little. Introverts spend a lot of time hiding in their own heads instead of getting themselves out of the jams that put them there, but extroverts can be just as hapless, with so many ways out there luring you to amuse and stimulate yourselves while getting you nowhere. If there is a key, overall "Way" to happiness demonstrated by the intrepid souls of Bikini Bottom, it is "Go figure."

Maybe this makes you nervous. Maybe you were taught always to think first and then do. That's fine, as long as you get to the doing. If you're having trouble pulling that trigger, just know it doesn't have to be so hard.

A classic example is depression. Not the long, drawn-out clinical type where we're not sure why it's there and it doesn't go away and we really need to see a shrink or our family physician, but that common bummed-out feeling that settles over us those days when things aren't going our way. It's really hard to think or feel our way out of a down mood like that. When we're depressed, we feel no energy to do anything. We sit around moping, and this makes it worse. If we force ourselves to get up and clean the closet or start the book report, we will feel better. We do what we would do if we felt like doing it, and the feeling follows the doing.

Face it, none of us is going to master the universe. And if we could, then what? We'd have to think of something else to do with our lives. The fun lies in trying to master the universe, just going at it, figuring out the parts important to our lives and acting on what we learn to make ourselves happier. That's what SpongeBob and his friends do, and we can do it, too.